T0220397

Getting Started with Ethereum

A Step-by-Step Guide to Becoming a Blockchain Developer

Davi Pedro Bauer

Apress®

Getting Started with Ethereum: A Step-by-Step Guide to Becoming a Blockchain Developer

Davi Pedro Bauer
Campo Bom, Rio Grande do Sul, Brazil

ISBN-13 (pbk): 978-1-4842-8044-7   ISBN-13 (electronic): 978-1-4842-8045-4
https://doi.org/10.1007/978-1-4842-8045-4

Copyright © 2022 by Davi Pedro Bauer

Managing Director, Apress Media LLC: Welmoed Spahr
Acquisitions Editor: Spandana Chatterjee
Coordinating Editor: Mark Powers
Copy Editor: Kim Wimpsett

Cover designed by eStudioCalamar

Cover image by Desmond Marshall on Unsplash (www.unsplash.com)

Distributed to the book trade worldwide by Apress Media, LLC, 1 New York Plaza, New York, NY 10004, U.S.A. Phone 1-800-SPRINGER, fax (201) 348-4505, e-mail orders-ny@springer-sbm.com, or visit www.springeronline.com. Apress Media, LLC is a California LLC and the sole member (owner) is Springer Science + Business Media Finance Inc (SSBM Finance Inc). SSBM Finance Inc is a **Delaware** corporation.

For information on translations, please e-mail booktranslations@springernature.com; for reprint, paperback, or audio rights, please e-mail bookpermissions@springernature.com.

Apress titles may be purchased in bulk for academic, corporate, or promotional use. eBook versions and licenses are also available for most titles. For more information, reference our Print and eBook Bulk Sales web page at www.apress.com/bulk-sales.

Any source code or other supplementary material referenced by the author in this book is available to readers on GitHub (https://github.com/Apress). For more detailed information, please visit www.apress.com/source-code.

Printed on acid-free paper

Table of Contents

About the Author

 **Davi Pedro Bauer** has more than 20 years of experience in the IT sector with experience in analysis and systems development. He has been working with agile methods since 2009, where he participated in agile adoption programs in multidisciplinary teams, supporting the implementation of processes and practices such as Scrum and Kanban, as well as the launch of new digital products for web and mobile platforms. Since 2016, he has been studying topics related to blockchain, such as cryptocurrencies, asset tokenization, smart contracts, and decentralized applications (DApps), and since 2019, he has been working with DevSecOps from code to infrastructure.

About the Technical Reviewer

 **Prasanth Sahoo** is a thought leader, an adjunct professor, a technical speaker, and a full-time practitioner in blockchain, DevOps, cloud, and agile working for PDI Software. He was awarded the "Blockchain and Cloud Expert of the Year Award 2019" from TCS Global Community for his knowledge sharing within academic services to the community. He is passionate about driving digital technology initiatives through coaching, mentoring, and grooming. Prasanth has a patent under his name, and to date, he has interacted with more than 50,000 professionals, mostly within the technical domain. He is a working group member in the Blockchain Council, CryptoCurrency Certification Consortium, Scrum Alliance, Scrum Organization, and International Institute of Business Analysis.

Introduction

This book is a step-by-step guide for everyone who wants to get started as an Ethereum developer. It was designed for those who have never programmed anything in the blockchain and want to get started.

I will cover everything from the basic requirements of installation to writing, testing, and deploying smart contracts. I will also cover topics such as IPFS, Filecoin, ENS, Chainlink, Truffle, Ganache, OpenZeppelin, Pinata, Fleek, Infura, MetaMask, and OpenSea, among others.

In Chapter 1, I will go through all the necessary requirements to start the activities described in this book. It covers software and tools such as Docker, Truffle, Ganache, MetaMask, and Infura.

In Chapter 2, you will learn how to create a basic Solidity project using the VS Code extension and then compile and deploy the smart contract to a local blockchain.

In Chapter 3, you will learn how to code smart contracts to create your own coin and deploy it to a local blockchain. Fungible tokens are interchangeable, so they are perfect to solve problems such as double spending. You will also be able to add this token to your own wallet and send it to different wallets, as well as send other coins that you already have.

In Chapter 4, you will learn how to create a unit test file for a smart contract, as well as write test assertions, run the unit tests, and check the unit test results.

In Chapter 5, you will be able to create smart contracts for badge tokens. You can use badge tokens, also known as NFTs, to represent physical things in the virtual world, such as digital collectibles, game items, digital art, etc. Each NFT token is unique and can have a unique value.

In this chapter, you will learn how to code the smart contract with the help of the OpenZeppelin library. You will also create the badge and add it to IPFS node. After that, you will learn to pin it so it is available for everyone, everywhere. Next, you will learn how to migrate the contract to different environments such as a local blockchain using Ganache and testnets using Infura. Finally, you will learn how to sell your own NFT on OpenSea.

In Chapter 6, we will cover different ways to fund your wallet using faucets. This part is important because you will need some ether in your wallet in order to pay for the transaction. Most of the examples will be deployed on testnets so you won't need real money to execute them.

In Chapter 7, you will learn how to create and save files on a decentralized file system. I also cover some tools such as a browser extension that will help you manage the node, as well as Pinata to help you pin your files remotely instead of keeping them locally. In addition, you will be able to host your own site on IPFS using Fleek.

In Chapter 8, I will cover ways to preserve files on a local node. The idea behind Filecoin is the same of IPFS, with the difference that Filecoin has an incentive mechanism and incentive nodes to preserve files. Filecoin was built on top of IPFS.

In Chapter 9, you will learn how to register a custom domain on the Ethereum Name System. You can use it to host a site under this domain name or even as a domain for your wallet to receive cryptos, tokens, or NFTs.

In Chapter 10, I will cover use cases where you need to pull data from off-chain using oracles. You will learn how to use price feeds and then crypto prices inside smart contracts.

In Chapter 11, you will learn how to create a simple project to connect to Web3 using the .NET platform and how to retrieve data from the blockchain to display wallet balances.

Chapter 12 concludes the book.

CHAPTER 1

Getting Started

In this chapter, I'll explain what Ethereum is and take you through the installations you'll need to perform before you can start using it.

What Is Ethereum?

Ethereum solves problems that go beyond Bitcoin. When developing decentralized applications, we need a platform where we can code not only coins but a wide variety of solutions.

Ethereum is a platform that allows you to code smart contracts in the Solidity language. Using it, you can compile your code into bytecode to be interpreted by the Ethereum Virtual Machine (EVM).

This virtual machine will interpret the instructions contained in the bytecode of your smart contract and will create a new state based on the rules described in the contract. It's like you have a state machine in your hand, where with every new state update, a new record is updated on the blockchain.

A virtual machine like EVM consumes resources, so you need a mechanism that generates incentives for more people to be nodes on the network while also preventing spam attacks. Because of this, an element called *gas* is required for the actions to be executed.

© Davi Pedro Bauer 2022
D. P. Bauer, *Getting Started with Ethereum*, https://doi.org/10.1007/978-1-4842-8045-4_1

To secure gas, you must first have *ether*, which is the currency of the Ethereum network. You use gas to pay for computing, so think of it as the cost of using the system. You will need gas to perform most of the activities described in this book.

The Ethereum platform allows you to build decentralized applications, which are applications where the source code is immutable and the data is impossible to change after writing. This opens up a range of new solutions, such as voting, supply chain, and decentralized finance, among others.

The best way to learn is by coding, so let's get started.

Installing Visual Studio Code

Before you can start using Ethereum, you'll need to install some software. First is Visual Studio Code,[1] an open source code editor that includes features for debugging, task execution, and version management. It provides developers with only the tools they need for a fast code-build-debug cycle, leaving more complicated processes to full-featured IDEs like Visual Studio IDE.

You can download it for free for different platforms like Windows, Linux, and Mac. All exercises in the book were based on the use of this tool.

Installing Docker

Docker[2] is a free and open platform for creating, delivering, and executing applications. Docker allows you to decouple your apps from your infrastructure, allowing you to deploy software more quickly. Docker allows you to manage your infrastructure in the same manner that you

---

[1] https://code.visualstudio.com
[2] https://docs.docker.com/get-docker/

control your apps. By utilizing Docker's techniques for fast shipping, testing, and deploying code, you may substantially shorten the time between developing code and executing it in production. You will need Docker to be started before compiling using Truffle.

Installing the Blockchain Dev Kit Extension on VS Code

The Blockchain Developer Kit for Ethereum[3] was designed for both new users of Ethereum and those who are already familiar with the process. One of the primary goals is to assist users in creating a project structure for these smart contracts; it also helps users compile and build the assets, deploy the assets to blockchain endpoints, and perform contract debugging.[4]

Installing the Extension

Go to Extensions and search for *Blockchain Development Kit for Ethereum*. Click the extension created by Microsoft; it will usually be the first one (Figure 1-1).

---

[3] https://marketplace.visualstudio.com/items?itemName=AzBlockchain.azure-blockchain

[4] https://www.youtube.com/watch?v=WIUppKQhtKk

3

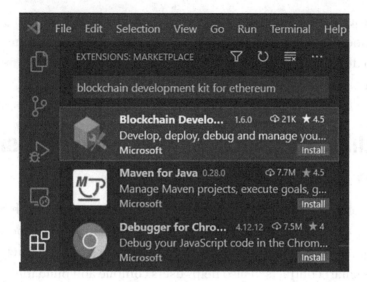

Figure 1-1. *Installing the Blockchain Development Kit for Ethereum*

Click Install and wait for the installation to finish. That's done!

Installing Truffle

Truffle[5] is an Ethereum development environment, testing framework, and asset pipeline that aims to make life easier for Ethereum developers. We will use this tool throughout the book.[6]

Installing Truffle

Go to the terminal window and install the Truffle package.

```
$ npm install -g truffle
```

---

[5] https://www.trufflesuite.com/truffle
[6] https://www.youtube.com/watch?v=mE3_3wL5-jI

Checking Truffle Installation

Now you can check whether the installation completed successfully. If you see the result shown in Figure 1-2, the installation was successful.

```
$ truffle
```

```
davi@DAVI-LATITUDE MINGW64 /c/blockchain/getstarted (master)
$ truffle
Truffle v5.2.6 - a development framework for Ethereum

Usage: truffle <command> [options]

Commands:
  build     Execute build pipeline (if configuration present)
  compile   Compile contract source files
  config    Set user-level configuration options
  console   Run a console with contract abstractions and commands available
  create    Helper to create new contracts, migrations and tests
  db        Database interface commands
  debug     Interactively debug any transaction on the blockchain
  deploy    (alias for migrate)
  develop   Open a console with a local development blockchain
  exec      Execute a JS module within this Truffle environment
  help      List all commands or provide information about a specific command
  init      Initialize new and empty Ethereum project
  install   Install a package from the Ethereum Package Registry
  migrate   Run migrations to deploy contracts
  networks  Show addresses for deployed contracts on each network
  obtain    Fetch and cache a specified compiler
  opcode    Print the compiled opcodes for a given contract
  publish   Publish a package to the Ethereum Package Registry
  run       Run a third-party command
  test      Run JavaScript and Solidity tests
  unbox     Download a Truffle Box, a pre-built Truffle project
  version   Show version number and exit
  watch     Watch filesystem for changes and rebuild the project automatically

See more at http://trufflesuite.com/docs
```

Figure 1-2. *Truffle command output result*

Installing the Ganache CLI

Ganache[7] is a personal blockchain that allows for the rapid development of the Ethereum and Corda distributed applications. Ganache can be used throughout the development cycle, allowing you to develop, deploy, and test your DApps in a secure and deterministic environment.[8]

Installing Ganache

Go to the terminal window and install the Ganache command line.

```
npm install -g ganache-cli
```

Starting Ganache Locally

Start the Ganache CLI on 127.0.0.1:8545 using the following command:

```
ganache-cli
```

Using this command, in addition to starting Ganache locally, it will generate ten accounts with their respective public and private keys so that you can use them for test purposes (Figure 1-3).

---

[7] https://www.trufflesuite.com/ganache

[8] https://www.youtube.com/watch?v=fbQH6pzfXig

```
davi@DAVI-LATITUDE MINGW64 /c/blockchain/getstarted (master)
$ ganache-cli
Ganache CLI v6.12.2 (ganache-core: 2.13.2)

Available Accounts
==================
(0) 0x6561f53E2c87E556b6f09BFf4799B3b2ea52Df3C (100 ETH)
(1) 0x4dD054592aB56a02F556801d9d25f4c21a79375a (100 ETH)
(2) 0x5D6F7D893DD4cd3f210bE411A8a080806CD497Ba (100 ETH)
(3) 0x919E866EdF19CA91abeC4Fd64A5b234180364ECD (100 ETH)
(4) 0x164b46F6ED93D3aaAb02258FbF45d00FDB388CB7 (100 ETH)
(5) 0x1ed6CB8Dff561C7124687A8e208041ec7dA326aA (100 ETH)
(6) 0x5e574182b073B1e071852eDC5d29c4591A14564E (100 ETH)
(7) 0xC080e81AB25f6790a3D0bFfab17e86B557e74d41 (100 ETH)
(8) 0x78759E4c5E0b8803D77fC46FBA0e15Ad85D00B42 (100 ETH)
(9) 0x91B49E68614E36CC6FdcDc22bA1d3207c0e9cf52 (100 ETH)
```

Figure 1-3. *Accounts generated by Ganache*

Installing and Setting Up MetaMask Wallet

MetaMask[9] is a browser extension that allows you to access Ethereum-enabled distributed applications, or DApps. The add-on injects the Ethereum Web3 API[10] into the JavaScript context of every website, allowing DApps to read from the blockchain.[11]

When a DApp wants to make a transaction and publish it to the blockchain, MetaMask gives the user a secure interface to evaluate the transaction before approving or rejecting it through private keys, local client wallets, and hardware wallets like Trezor.[12]

---

[9] https://metamask.io

[10] https://web3js.readthedocs.io

[11] https://youtu.be/Bj6IozLyVxw

[12] https://trezor.io

Installing the Wallet

Go to `https://metamask.io` and click Install MetaMask. Click Add to Brave or your browser name and then click "Add extension." Finally, click "Get started."

Configuring the Wallet

Click "Create a wallet" and then click "No thanks" (if you prefer, click "I agree" instead). Define the password that you will use to open your wallet and then confirm the password. Agree to the terms of use. Finally, click Create. Now you can back up your secret phrase (you can also do it later). For now, click "Remind me later." Your wallet is done!

Accessing Your Wallet

Click Extensions and pin MetaMask to your bar. Now, click the MetaMask icon, and your wallet will be shown.

Discovering Your Wallet Address

Click the three dots on the upper-right side and then click "Account details." Notice that you can see your wallet address in hash format and in QR code format. You can also copy your wallet address by clicking the account name. That's it!

Create an Account on Infura

Infura[13] delivers the tools and infrastructure that enable developers to rapidly transition their blockchain application from testing to scaled deployment, all while maintaining simple, dependable access to Ethereum and IPFS. A well-known use case that uses Infura as a data interface is Uniswap.[14,15]

Creating a New Account

Go to Infura[16] and click "Get started for free." Enter your email and password and then click "Sign up." A verification email will be sent to your address (Figure 1-4).

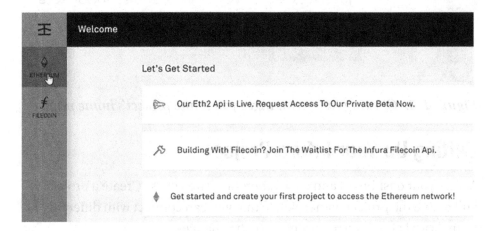

Figure 1-4. *The Infura welcome page you will see after logging in*

---

[13] https://infura.io

[14] https://uniswap.org

[15] https://www.youtube.com/watch?v=NcKMBgNsBuw

[16] https://infura.io

Check your email and confirm your account by clicking the verification link. After that, you will be redirected to your dashboard. Click the Ethereum tab in the left menu.

Now that your account is created, you can start setting up a new project (Figure 1-5).

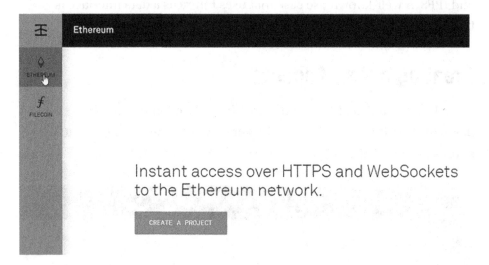

Figure 1-5. *Clicking Ethereum takes you to the project's home page*

Setting Up Your Infura Project

Access your dashboard and click Ethereum. Then click "Create a project" and define the project name. Notice that you can connect with different testnets and also to the mainnet. Save the changes.

After the project is created, information about the ID, secret, and endpoint for the connection is provided (Figure 1-6).

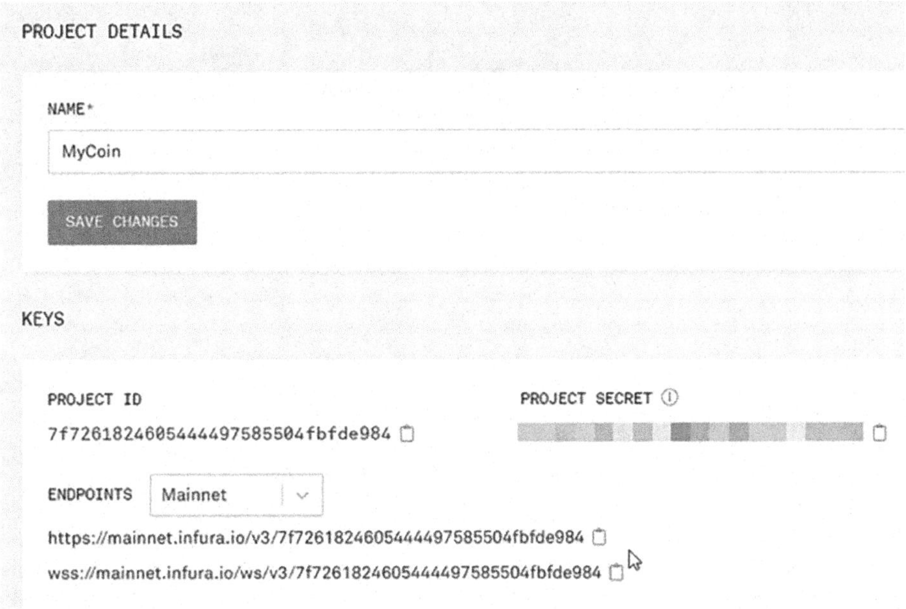

PROJECT DETAILS

NAME*

MyCoin

SAVE CHANGES

KEYS

PROJECT ID

7f726182460544497585504fbfde984

PROJECT SECRET ⓘ

ENDPOINTS   Mainnet

https://mainnet.infura.io/v3/7f726182460544497585504fbfde984
wss://mainnet.infura.io/ws/v3/7f726182460544497585504fbfde984

Figure 1-6. *Infura project details page*

Summary

In this chapter, you learned what Ethereum is and how to install the necessary software to begin developing smart contracts.

In the next chapter, you will explore Solidity and learn how to set up your first project in this language.

CHAPTER 2

Solidity

Solidity is an object-oriented, high-level programming language that is used to construct smart contracts that automate blockchain transactions. The language was proposed in 2014 by Gavin Wood and developed by participants of the Ethereum project. Solidity was influenced by C++, Python, and JavaScript, so you will find similar language structures as in those languages. The language is primarily used to build smart contracts on the Ethereum blockchain, but it can also be used to create smart contracts on other blockchains.

Solidity, being a high-level language, eliminates the need to type code in ones and zeros. It makes it much easier for people to create programs in a form that they can comprehend, by combining letters and numbers.

Because Solidity is statically typed, each variable must be specified by the user. Data types enable the compiler to validate variable usage. Solidity data types are often divided into two categories: value types and reference types.

The Ethereum ecosystem is distinctive in that it can be used by a wide range of cryptocurrencies and decentralized apps. On Ethereum, smart contracts enable the creation of solutions for all types of enterprises and organizations.

© Davi Pedro Bauer 2022
D. P. Bauer, *Getting Started with Ethereum*, https://doi.org/10.1007/978-1-4842-8045-4_2

At the end of this chapter, you will be able to do the following:

- Create a basic Solidity project using the VS Code extension

- Compile the contract

- Deploy the contract to a local blockchain

Getting Started with the Solidity Project on VS Code

Ethereum is the most often utilized platform for smart contracts. Ethereum is the first programmable blockchain in the world. It enables the creation of smart contracts to aid in the transfer of digital assets such as ether.

Solidity[1] is the language you will use to build contracts; it is Turing-complete, which means that it allows you to build complex contracts in a well-defined and coded manner.

Creating a New Project

Select "View ➤ Command Palette" and then click "Blockchain: New Solidity Project" (Figure 2-1). Finally, click "Create basic project" (Figure 2-2).

Figure 2-1. *New Solidity project*

---

[1] https://soliditylang.org

Figure 2-2. *Creating a basic project*

Select a folder where the project will be scaffolded and wait for the project to be created. Make sure the project structure was created, as shown in Figure 2-3.

Figure 2-3. *Solidity project structure created*

Compiling the Project

Right-click the `HelloBlockchain.sol` file, select "Build contracts," and wait for contracts to be built.

Deploying to a Development Blockchain

Right-click the `HelloBlockchain.sol` file, select "Deploy contracts," and then select Development 127.0.0.1:8545. Wait for the contracts to be deployed to the blockchain development network. That's it!

Summary

In this chapter, you learned what Solidity is, and you created, compiled, and deployed your first smart contract.

In the next chapter, you will explore the ERC-20 token standard and learn how to create and deploy to development, test, and production environments.

CHAPTER 3

ERC-20: Fungible Tokens

Fungible tokens are tokens where each unit has the same value, in the same way as fiat currency. This means you can exchange one unit of this currency for another unit of this currency for the same amount. Thinking about replicating this behavior on the blockchain, Fabian Vogelsteller and Vitalik Buterin proposed the creation of ERC-20, "Ethereum Request for Comments 20," in November 2015 to create a simple format for Ethereum-based tokens. These tokens work within the Ethereum blockchain and are able to interact with other cryptocurrencies on the network. In this chapter, you will create simple contracts in the ERC-20 standard and learn how to deploy them to test and production networks.

At the end of this chapter, you will be able to do the following:

- Write a simple contract in the ERC-20 standard.

- Write a fixed supply contract.

- Inherit key implementations with OpenZeppelin.

- Compile the contract using Truffle.

- Start a localhost blockchain using Ganache.

- Deploy the existing contract to Ganache.

- Configure MetaMask to connect to Ganache.

© Davi Pedro Bauer 2022

D. P. Bauer, *Getting Started with Ethereum*, https://doi.org/10.1007/978-1-4842-8045-4_3

- Add the deployed token contract to your
  MetaMask wallet.

- Migrate the contract to Ganache.

- Transfer tokens between accounts.

- Add Polygon Mumbai to MetaMask networks.

- Activate the Polygon add-on on Infura.

- Configure the private key to sign the contract.

- Deploy the smart contract on Polygon Mumbai.

- Add the Polygon mainnet to MetaMask networks.

- Configure the network to use the Polygon mainnet.

- Deploy the smart contract on the Polygon mainnet.

- Verify the smart contract on the Polygon mainnet.

Write a Simple ERC-20 Token Using OpenZeppelin

Let's use Truffle to develop a simple ERC-20 Ethereum[1] smart contract and then import the OpenZeppelin contracts library.

OpenZeppelin is an open source and auditable library that allows you to reuse code from more common implementations, thus serving as an initial code base that is always the same. Using OpenZeppelin allows you to focus more on coding the business need rather than repeating unnecessary code.

We will use the OpenZeppelin library in this example and in subsequent chapters of this book.

---

[1] https://ethereum.org/en/developers/docs/standards/tokens/erc-20/

18

Tokens can represent virtually everything in Ethereum, such as the following:

- Reputation points in an online platform

- Skills of a character in a game

- Lottery tickets

- Financial assets like a share in a company

- A fiat currency like USD

- An ounce of gold

Preparing the Environment

Initialize Truffle using the following command:

```
$ truffle init
```

Now, initialize the project folder.

```
$ npm init
```

Finally, install the OpenZeppelin contracts package.

```
$ npm install @openzeppelin/contracts
```

Writing the Contract

Create a new file under the contracts folder with the name
ERC20MinerReward.sol. Add the license directive, define the Solidity
minimum version, and import the OpenZeppelin ERC-20 contract library.
Finally, define the contract class, the contract constructor, the contract
name, and the contract symbol.

```
// SPDX-License-Identifier: MIT
pragma solidity ^0.8.0;

import "@openzeppelin/contracts/token/ERC20/ERC20.sol";

contract ERC20MinerReward is ERC20 {
    constructor() ERC20("MinerReward", "MRW"){}
}
```

Setting the Solidity Compiler Version

Copy the Solidity version used in this contract and then open `truffle-config.js`. Uncomment the `solc` block and set the Solidity version by pasting in the copied value.

```
compilers: {
    solc: {
        version: "0.8.0",
        docker: true,
        settings: {
            optimizer: {
                enabled: false,
                runs: 200
            },
            evmVersion: "byzantium"
        }
    }
},
```

Compiling the Contract

Now it is the time to compile the contract.

```
$ truffle compile
```

The contract was compiled successfully!

Verifying the Result

Notice that a new folder build/contract was created (Figure 3-1). The new contract is there!

Figure 3-1. *Truffle compile results*

Deploy the ERC-20 Token to the Ganache Development Blockchain

Ethereum Ganache is a local in-memory blockchain that is intended for development and testing. It mimics the characteristics of a real Ethereum network, including the availability of a number of accounts funded with test ether.

This is a nice way to deploy contracts before moving them to a main network. Using a development blockchain, you can focus on the implementation without worrying about spending real money to deploy the contracts.

Preparing the Migration

Create a new migration file named 2_deploy_contracts.js under the migrations folder. In the first line, add a reference to the smart contract and add an export function to deploy the smart contract (Figure 3-2).

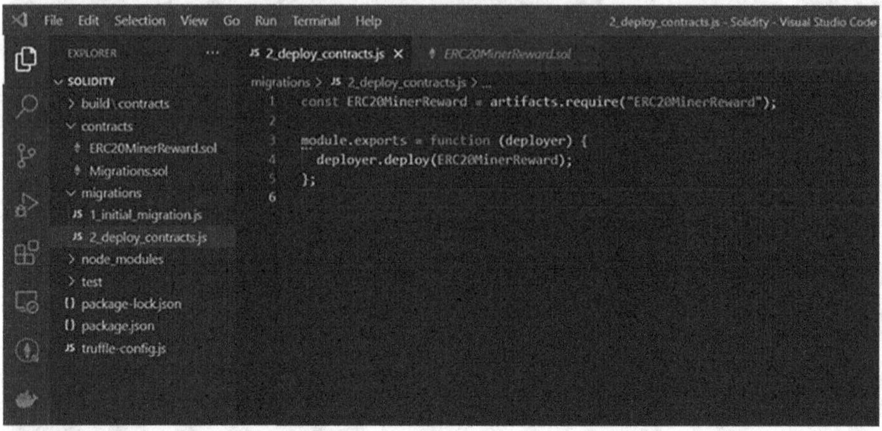

Figure 3-2. *New migration file*

Starting the Blockchain

Open a new terminal and start the Ganache blockchain.

```
$ ganache-cli
```

A new Ganache blockchain is listening on 127.0.0.1:8545.

Configuring the Blockchain Network

Open truffle-config.js and uncomment the development block from networks. Make sure the host and port are correct (Figure 3-3).

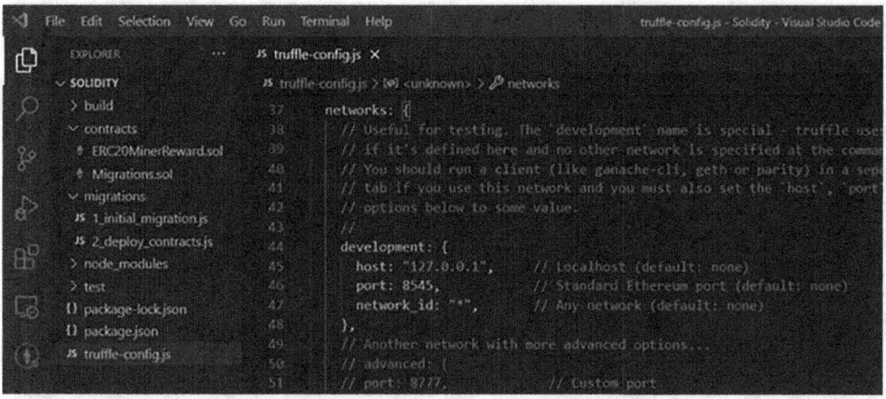

Figure 3-3. *Development network*

Deploying the Contract

Compile the contract using the following command:

```
$ truffle compile
```

Migrate the contract using the following command:

```
$ truffle migrate
```

The contract was deployed to the Ganache blockchain, and a contract address was created (Figure 3-4).

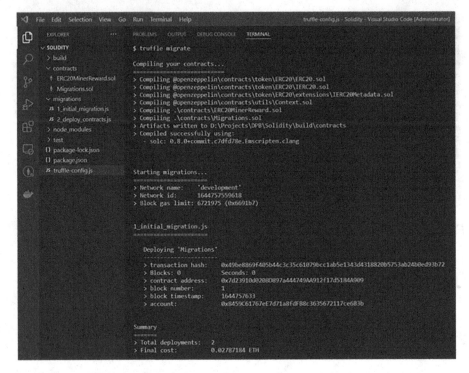

Figure 3-4. *Truffle migrate contract*

Adding Ganache to MetaMask Networks

Open the MetaMask extension and click the Network drop-down. Select the Custom RPC option and set the following fields, as shown in the Figure 3-5:

- Set the network name to **Localhost 8545**.

- Set the RPC URL to **http://localhost:8545**.

- Set the chain ID to **1337**.

- Set the currency symbol to **ETH**.

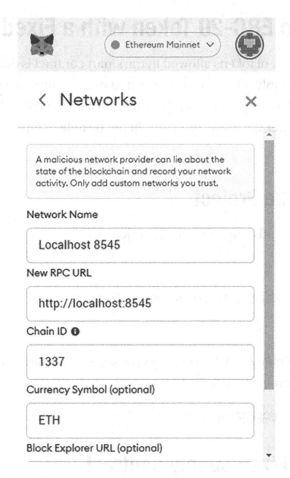

Figure 3-5. *MetaMask network configuration*

Adding the Token to a Wallet

Go to the Brave browser (or any browser compatible with MetaMask) and select the "Localhost 8585" network.

Click "Add token" and click "Custom token." Copy the contract address. Paste it into the "Token contract address" field.

The "Token symbol" and "Decimals of precision" fields are filled automatically. Click "Next" and click "Add token." The token was added to the MetaMask wallet. The token is there!

Create an ERC-20 Token with a Fixed Supply

The total number of tokens allowed in the smart contract is defined by ERC-20 fixed supply tokens. You cannot update the contract once it has been deployed to the blockchain. This means that your coin will have that fixed amount after deployed and you will not be able to fund with more coins later.

Creating the Project

Initialize a new and empty Ethereum project.

```
$ truffle init
```

Create a `package.json` file for your project.

```
$ npm init
```

Install the OpenZeppelin contracts package. It contains reusable smart contracts written in Solidity.

```
$ npm install @openzeppelin/contracts
```

Writing a Fixed Supply Contract

Create a new solidity file and do the following:

1. Include the license declaration (this is mandatory).

2. Define the Solidity minimum version.

3. Import the OpenZeppelin ERC-20 contract library.

4. Define the fixed supply contract class, inheriting from ERC-20.

5. Call the constructor, passing the name and symbol.

6. Assign the total supply to the sender address (who created the contract).

7. Override the decimals function.

8. Set the number of decimals that this token will have.

```solidity
// SPDX-License-Identifier: MIT
pragma solidity ^0.8.0;

import "@openzeppelin/contracts/token/ERC20/ERC20.sol";

contract ERC20FixedSupply is ERC20 {
    constructor() ERC20("Fixed", "FIX"){
        _mint(msg.sender, 1000);
    }

    function decimals() public view virtual override returns
    (uint8){
        return 0;
    }
}
```

Go to `truffle-config.js` and uncomment the solc block (Ctrl+;). Now, update the Solidity version number.

```javascript
compilers: {
    solc: {
        version: "0.8.0",
        docker: true,
        settings: {
            optimizer: {
                enabled: false,
                runs: 200
            },
```

```
        evmVersion: "byzantium"
    }
  }
},
```

Under the migrations folder, create a new file. Set the name to 2_deploy_contracts.sol.

```
$ touch migrations/2_deploy_contracts.sol
```

In this file, set the required method to your contract file and export a function to deploy the contract.

```
var ERC20FixedSupply = artifacts.require("./
ERC20FixedSupply.sol");

module.exports = function(deployer){
    deployer.deploy(ERC20FixedSupply);
}
```

Compiling the Contract

Now it is time to compile the contract.

```
$ truffle compile
```

The contract was compiled successfully!

Starting the Ganache Development Blockchain

Split the terminal view. Now, start the Ganache development blockchain on 127.0.0.1:8545.

```
$ ganache-cli
```

Go to `truffle-config.js`, and under `networks`, uncomment the development block.

```
networks: {
    development: {
        host: "127.0.0.1",
        port: 8545,
        network_id: "*"
    },
}
```

Migrating the Contract to Ganache

Run the `migrate` command to deploy contracts, as shown in Figure 3-6.

```
$ truffle migrate
```

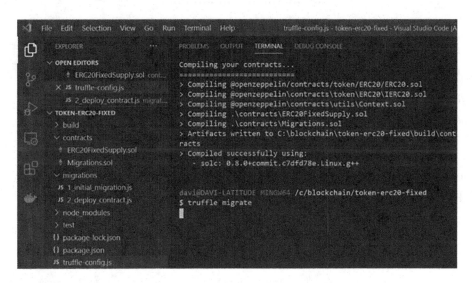

Figure 3-6. *VS Code: migrating the project using the truffle command line*

Before proceeding to the next section, copy the private key of the account that deployed the token.

Configuring MetaMask

Open MetaMask. Click your account and then click "Import account." In this step, paste the account private key. Click on "Import", as shown in Figure 3-7.

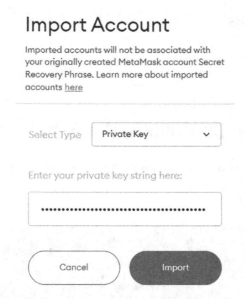

Figure 3-7. *MetaMask: importing an existing wallet using the seed phase*

Click the Networks list and then click Localhost:8545. Using the localhost network means you will be pointing your wallet to your local development blockchain, as shown in Figure 3-8.

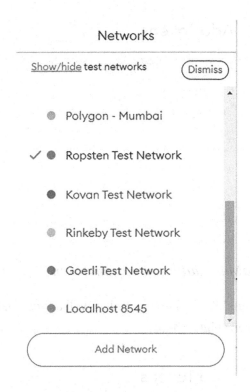

Figure 3-8. *MetaMask: network selection list*

Adding the Token to MetaMask

Click "Add token" and then select "Custom token." Paste in the token contract address and click "Next".

Adding a token is a matter of adding the contract public address of the created token. MetaMask will read the symbol and the number of decimal places automatically after that. Make sure you get the same result as shown in Figure 3-9.

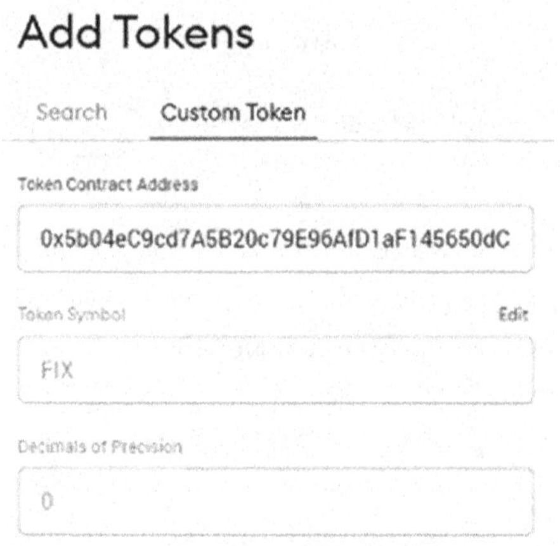

Add Tokens

Search   **Custom Token**

Token Contract Address

0x5b04eC9cd7A5B20c79E96AfD1aF145650dC

Token Symbol   Edit

FIX

Decimals of Precision

0

Figure 3-9. *MetaMask: adding a custom token*

Click "Add tokens." The token symbol as well as your balance will be shown on this screen (Figure 3-10).

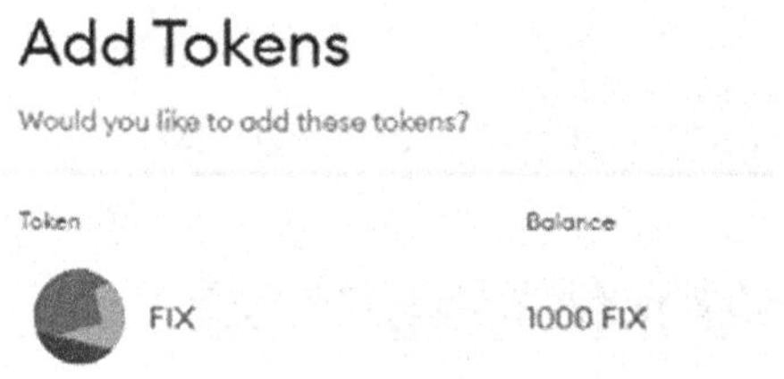

Add Tokens

Would you like to add these tokens?

Token   Balance

FIX   1000 FIX

Figure 3-10. *MetaMask: new custom token overview*

Now, go back to VS Code (see Figure 3-6 for the ganache-cli terminal view) and copy another account private key. Return to MetaMask and repeat the steps you did for the first account, including adding the token.

Transferring Tokens Between Accounts

Now, switch to the first imported account (the one that has all the tokens). Click "Send" and then click "Transfer between my accounts." Select the second created account. Enter **115 FIX** as the amount to transfer and click "Next". Finally, click "Confirm".

The transaction was sent, but it's in a pending state. Wait a moment for the transaction to be confirmed. Once that happens, the total number of tokens will be updated. Select the second imported account; now this account has 115 FIX!

Deploy the ERC-20 Token to a Testnet Using Infura

Infura can be used to deploy smart contracts to test networks such as Ropsten, Kovan, Rinkeby, Goerli, and also the mainnet. For the testnet, you will need to create a new project on Infura and have access to the wallet's private key, which you will use to deploy the contracts. To execute the contract creation transaction, this wallet must have an ether balance.

Installing the Prerequisites

Open a new terminal and install the fs package. Installing this package provides useful functionality to access and interact with the file system.

```
$ npm install fs
```

Now, install the wallet provider hdwallet package. This is used to sign transactions for addresses derived from a 12- or 24-word mnemonic.

```
$ npm install @truffle/hdwallet-provider@1.2.3
```

Setting Up Your Infura Project

Go to http://infura.io and access your dashboard. Click "Ethereum" and then click "Create a Project". Define the project name. Notice that you can connect with different testnets and also to the mainnet. Copy the project ID and save the changes.

Setting Up Your Smart Contract

Go to Visual Studio Code and open truffle-config.js. Uncomment the four constants: hdwalletprovider, infurakey, fs, and mnemonic. Paste the project ID as a value for the Infurakey constant. Uncomment the ropsten block. Make sure you are using the correct project ID in the ropsten endpoint.

```
const HDWalletProvider = require('@truffle/hdwallet-provider');
const infuraKey = "fj4jll3k.....";

const fs = require('fs');
const mnemonic = fs.readFileSync(".secret").toString().trim();
```

Configuring the Private Key

Go to the browser and open your MetaMask wallet connected to the Infura network. Click "*your account*" and then click "settings," and finally click "security & privacy" (Figure 3-11).

You have the option to view your seed phrase, but be aware that this information is sensitive and if someone has access to it, they will be able to restore your wallet and make use of your funds.

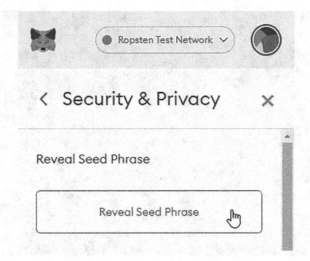

Figure 3-11. *MetaMask: revealing the seed phrase*

Click "Reveal Seed Phrase" and enter your wallet password to continue; then copy the private key.

Go back to Visual Studio Code (Figure 3-6) and create a new file named .secret. Paste the private key into this file. You can also create this file using the command line (Figure 3-12).

```
$ touch .secret
```

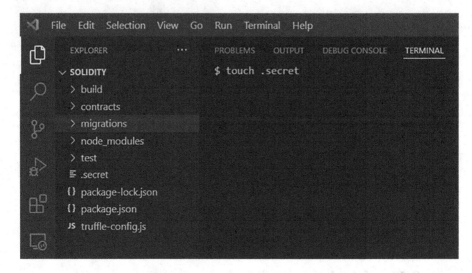

Figure 3-12. *Secret file*

Deploying the Smart Contract

Open the terminal and run the `migrate` command to deploy the contracts on the Ropsten network.

```
$ truffle migrate --network ropsten
```

Checking Your Wallet Balance

Go to your MetaMask wallet again and notice now that your balance has been reduced.

Verifying the Smart Contract on Etherscan

Open a new window and copy the contract address that was created in the deploy stage. Go to `https://ropsten.etherscan.io` and paste the contract address into the search field. Click the Find button. The smart contract is there!

The tokens were created and transferred to the wallet that created the contract. Click the Fixed (FIX) token link. Here you can see an overview of your newly created token.

Deploy the ERC-20 Token to the Polygon Testnet (Layer 2)

Polygon is a protocol and framework for building and connecting Ethereum-compatible blockchain networks. You can aggregate scalable solutions on Ethereum to support a multichain Ethereum ecosystem.

MATIC, the native token of Polygon, is an ERC-20 token running on the Ethereum blockchain. The tokens are used for payment services on Polygon and as a settlement currency between users who operate within the Polygon ecosystem.

Installing the Prerequisites

Open a new terminal and install the `fs` package, if you haven't already done so. This package provides a lot of useful functionality to access and interact with the file system.

```
$ npm install fs
```

Now, install the wallet provider `hdwallet` package, if you haven't already done so. It is used to sign transactions for addresses derived from a 12- or 24-word mnemonic.

```
$ npm install @truffle/hdwallet-provider@1.4.0
```

Adding Polygon Mumbai to MetaMask Networks

Open the MetaMask extension and click the Network drop-down. Then select the Custom RPC option. Set the following values, as shown in Figure 3-13:

- Set the network name to **Matic Testnet**.

- Set the RPC URL to **https://rpc-mumbai.matic-vigil.com**.

- Set the chain ID to **80001**.

- Set the currency symbol to **MATIC**.

- Set the Block Explorer URL to **https://explore-mumbai.maticvigil.com**.

Network Name

> Matic Testnet

New RPC URL

> https://rpc-mumbai.maticvigil.com

Chain ID ❶

> 80001

Currency Symbol (optional)

> MATIC

Block Explorer URL (optional)

> https://explorer-mumbai.maticvigil.com

Figure 3-13. *MetaMask: network configuration page*

Activating the Polygon Add-on on Infura

Go to https://infura.io/upgrade and click Select Addon in the Polygon PoS under Network Add-ons, as shown in Figure 3-14. The Polygon PoS is currently in beta version on Infura, and you need to activate it.

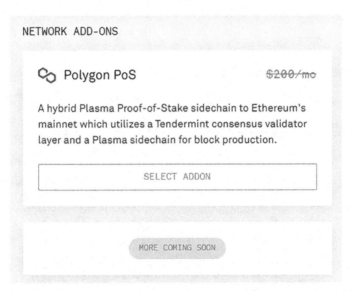

Figure 3-14. *Infura: Polygon PoS activation page*

After activating it, you will be redirected to the summary page. The free layer is limited to 100,000 requests a day. You will be asked to provide a credit card in order to confirm; as the total cost is zero, you will not be charged. If you agree, click Get Started Now. You should see a page similar to the one shown in Figure 3-15.

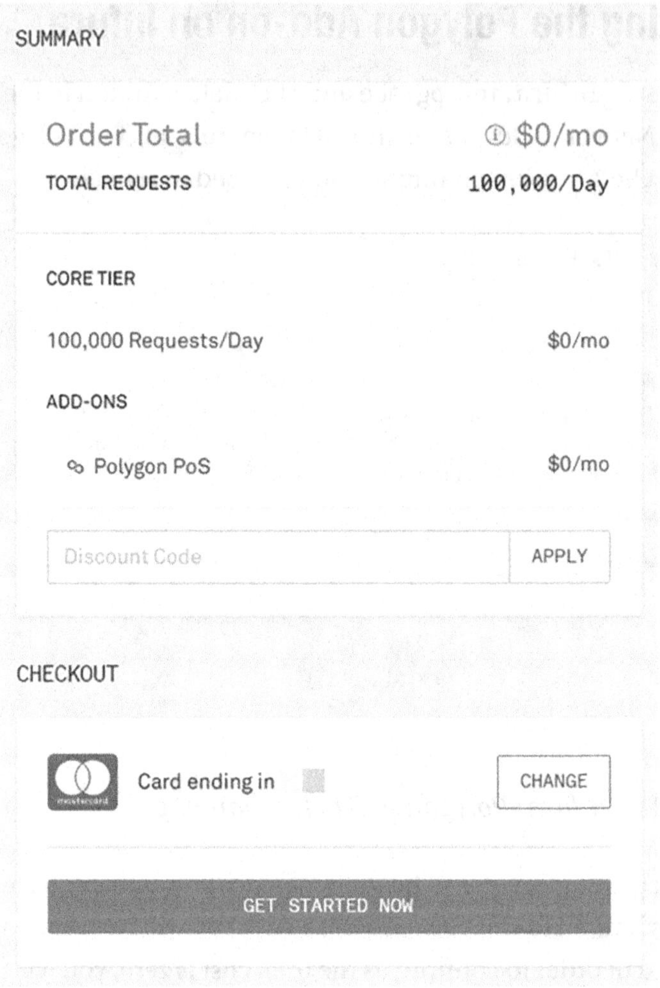

SUMMARY

Order Total   ⓘ $0/mo

TOTAL REQUESTS   100,000/Day

CORE TIER

100,000 Requests/Day $0/mo

ADD-ONS

    ∞ Polygon PoS $0/mo

Discount Code	APPLY

CHECKOUT

Card ending in ▓   CHANGE

GET STARTED NOW

Figure 3-15. *Infura: Summary page order after adding the Polygon PoS plugin*

Setting Up Your Infura Project

Make sure that you have a project already set up on Infura. If you haven't already, please follow the steps in Chapter 1.

Setting Up Your Smart Contract

Go to Visual Studio Code and open `truffle-config.js`. Uncomment the four constants: `hdwalletprovider`, `infurakey`, `fs`, and `mnemonic` and *p*aste the project ID as a value for `infurakey` constant.

```
const HDWalletProvider = require('@truffle/hdwallet-provider');
const infuraKey = "fj4jll3k.....";

const fs = require('fs');
const mnemonic = fs.readFileSync(".secret").toString().trim();
```

Configuring the Network (Using the Matic Endpoint)

The first way to connect to a Polygon network is using the Matic network. Now, create a `matic_testnet` configuration under `networks` in the `truffle-config.js` file and set the following values:

- Set the wallet URL to `https://rpc-mumbai.matic-vigil.com`.

- Set `network_id` to 80001.

```
matic_testnet: {
  provider: () => new HDWalletProvider(mnemonic, `https://rpc-
  mumbai.maticvigil.com`),
  network_id: 80001,
  confirmations: 2,
  timeoutBlocks: 200,
  skipDryRun: true
},
```

Configuring the Network (Using the Infura Endpoint)

Another way to connect to the Polygon network is using the Infura endpoint. Create a `matic_testnet` configuration under `networks` and set the following values:

- Set the wallet URL to `https://polygon-mumbai.infura.io/v3/${infuraKey}`.

- Set `network_id` to 80001.

```
matic_testnet: {
  provider: () => new HDWalletProvider(mnemonic, `https://
  polygon-mumbai.infura.io/v3/${infuraKey}`),
  network_id: 80001,
  confirmations: 2,
  timeoutBlocks: 200,
  skipDryRun: true,
  chainId: 80001,
  networkCheckTimeout: 1000000
},
```

To use the Polygon network, you will need to activate the network add-on.

Configuring the Private Key

Go to the browser and open your MetaMask wallet connected to the Infura network. Click "*your account*" and then click "settings." Finally, click "security & privacy," as you can see in Figure 3-16.

You have the option to view your seed phrase, but be aware that this information is sensitive, and if someone has access to it, they will be able to restore your wallet and make use of your funds.

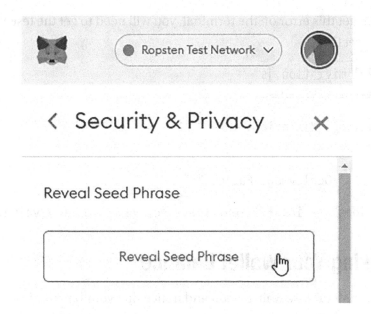

Figure 3-16. *MetaMask: revealing the seed phrase*

Click Reveal Seed Phrase and enter your wallet password to continue. Copy the private key.

Go back to VS Code (on the `ganache-cli` terminal view) and create a new file named `.secret`. Paste the private secret recovery phrase on this file.

Deploying the Smart Contract

Run the `migrate` command to deploy contracts to the `matic_testnet` network.

```
$ truffle migrate --network matic_testnet
```

If you get this error on the terminal, you will need to get the test MATIC from Faucet first.

```
1_initial_migration.js
======================

   Deploying 'Migrations'
   ----------------------

Error:   *** Deployment Failed ***

"Migrations" -- insufficient funds for gas * price + value.
```

Checking Your Wallet Balance

Go to your MetaMask wallet again and notice that your balance has been reduced. This happens because you need to pay for each contract deployment. It has an equivalent cost in gas, and that cost is calculated according to the instructions you use inside a smart contract. This means that the more machine processing you need, the higher the gas cost for you to execute this contract. You can find a more detailed explanation of how this is calculated in the Ethereum yellow paper.

Verifying the Smart Contract on PolygonScan

Copy the contract address that was created in the deploy (this address will be shown in the console after `truffle migrate` has finished running) and go to `https://mumbai.polygonscan.com`. Paste the contract address in the search field and click the Find button. The smart contract is there!

The tokens were created and transferred to the wallet that created the contract. Now, click the Fixed (FIX) token link, and here you can see the overview of your newly created token!

Deploy the ERC-20 Token to the Polygon Mainnet (Layer 2)

The mainnet network is used for real transactions, while testnets are used for testing smart contracts and decentralized applications (DApps). Polygon is used as a second layer and gained popularity because of the transaction cost that are lower than the mainnet.

Adding the Polygon Mainnet to MetaMask Networks

Open the MetaMask extension, click the Network drop-down, and then select the Custom RPC option. Set the following values as shown in Figure 3-17:

- Set the network name to **Matic Mainnet**.

- Set the RPC URL to **https://rpc-mainnet.matic-vigil.com**.

- Set the chain ID to **137**.

- Set the currency symbol to **MATIC**.

- Set the Block Explorer URL to **https://explore-mainnet.maticvigil.com**.

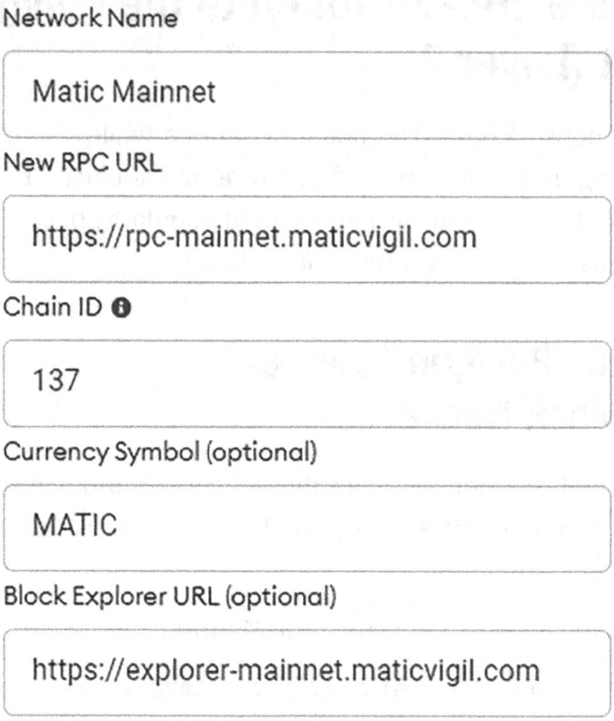

Network Name

Matic Mainnet

New RPC URL

https://rpc-mainnet.maticvigil.com

Chain ID ❶

137

Currency Symbol (optional)

MATIC

Block Explorer URL (optional)

https://explorer-mainnet.maticvigil.com

Figure 3-17. MetaMask: network configuration page

Configuring the Network (Using the Infura Endpoint)

Another way to connect to the Polygon network is to use the Infura endpoint. Create a `matic_mainnet` configuration under `networks` and set the following values:

- Set the wallet URL to `https://polygon-mainnet.infura.io/v3/${infuraKey}`.

- Set `network_id` to 137.

```
matic_mainnet: {
  provider: () => new HDWalletProvider(mnemonic, `https://
  polygon-mainnet.infura.io/v3/${infuraKey}`),
  network_id: 137,
  gasPrice: 100000000,
  confirmations: 2,
  timeoutBlocks: 200,
  skipDryRun: true,
  chainId: 137,
  networkCheckTimeout: 1000000
},
```

Deploying the Smart Contract

Run the `migrate` command to deploy contracts to the `matic_mainnet` network.

```
$ truffle migrate --network matic_mainnet
```

Checking Your Wallet Balance

Go to your MetaMask wallet again and notice that your balance has been reduced.

Verifying the Smart Contract on PolygonScan

Copy the contract address that was created in the deployment and go to PolygonScan.[2] Paste the contract address in the search field and click the Find button. The smart contract is there!

---

[2]`https://polygonscan.com`

The tokens were created and transferred to the wallet that created the contract. Now, click the Fixed (FIX) token link, and here you can see the overview of your newly created token.

Summary

In this chapter, you learned what the ERC-20 token standard is and learned how to create and deploy fungible tokens to Ganache to the testnet and mainnet networks on the Ethereum and Polygon blockchains.

In the next chapter, you will explore unit tests on smart contracts and learn how to write your first unit test.

CHAPTER 4

Unit Tests for Smart Contracts

Unit tests are used to test code execution scenarios and ensure that they behave as expected. Crucially, unit tests allow you to refactor code and make new changes without breaking existing behaviors.

In smart contracts, unit tests are even more important, as once the contract is deployed, it is no longer possible to fix it unless you deploy a new contract. Because of this, it is of fundamental importance that you incorporate unit tests into all the smart contracts you write, looking for as much coverage as possible.

In this chapter, you will learn how to write unit tests using Mocha as the test runner and Chai as the assertion library.

At the end of this chapter, you will be able to do the following:

- Create a unit test file

- Write unit tests for the smart contract

- Write test assertions

- Run the unit tests

- Check the unit test results

© Davi Pedro Bauer 2022
D. P. Bauer, *Getting Started with Ethereum*, https://doi.org/10.1007/978-1-4842-8045-4_4

Writing Unit Tests for ERC-20 Smart Contracts

Truffle has an automated testing framework by default, making it considerably easier to test your contracts. This framework allows you to create basic and manageable tests in a variety of ways. Let's start coding our first unit test.

Creating a New Unit Test File

Open a new terminal and execute the following command:

```
$ truffle create test erc20FixedSupply
```

Writing a Test for the Total Supply Contract

In the file ERC20FixedSupply.js, write a new test to assert that the contract was created with a fixed supply of 1,000 coins.

```
const erc20FixedSupply = artifacts.require("erc20FixedSupply");

contract("erc20FixedSupply", function () {
    it("should assert true", async function() {
        let token = await erc20FixedSupply.deployed();
        let name = await token.name();
        assert.equal(name, 'Fixed');
    });

    it("should return total supply of 1000", async function() {
        const instance = await erc20FixedSupply.deployed();
        const totalSupply = await instance.totalSupply();

        assert.equal(totalSupply, 1000);
    });
});
```

Test using the following command:

```
$ truffle test --network development
```

Make sure that the test will pass.

Writing Test Assertions for the Balance Contract

In the file ERC20FixedSupply.js, add one more test to assert that the balance is correct after a new transfer is made between two accounts.

```
it("should transfer 150 FIX", async function(){
    const instance = await erc20FixedSupply.deployed();
    await instance.transfer(account[1], 150);

    const balanceAccount0 = await instance.balanceOf
    (accounts[0]);
    const balanceAccount1 = await instance.balanceOf
    (accounts[1]);

    assert.equal(balanceAccount0.toNumber(), 850);
    assert.equal(balanceAccount1.toNumber(), 150);
});
```

Running the Unit Tests

Now, execute the test again.

```
$ truffle test --network development
```

Once again, make sure that all the tests pass. If the unit test has passed, a green check mark will appear; otherwise, a red x symbol will appear.

Checking the Unit Test Results

Make sure you get the same output as shown in Figure 4-1.

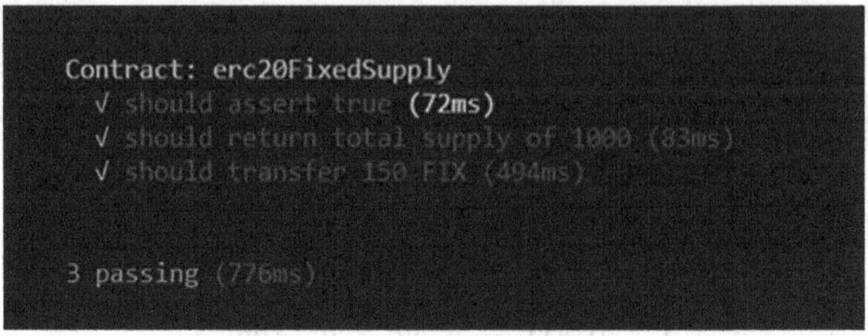

Figure 4-1. *VS Code: unit test results succeed*

Try to change some values like the account balance and see how the results change from pass to fail, as shown in Figure 4-2.

```
it("should transfer 150 FIX", async function(){
    const instance = await erc20FixedSupply.deployed();
    await instance.transfer("account[1]", 150);

    const balanceAccount0 = await instance.balanceOf
    (accounts[0]);
    const balanceAccount1 = await instance.balanceOf
    (accounts[1]);

    assert.equal(balanceAccount0.toNumber(), 750);
    assert.equal(balanceAccount1.toNumber(), 250);
});
```

```
Contract: erc20FixedSupply
  √ should assert true (51ms)
  √ should return total supply of 1000 (51ms)
  1) should transfer 150 FIX


  Events emitted during test:
  ---------------------------
1) Contract: erc20FixedSupply
     should transfer 150 FIX:

     AssertionError: expected 850 to equal 750
     + expected - actual

     -850
     +750

     at Context.<anonymous> (test\erc20_fixed_supply.js:24:14)
     at processTicksAndRejections (node:internal/process/task_queues:96:5)
```

Figure 4-2. *VS Code: unit test results failed*

Summary

In this chapter, you learned the importance of writing unit tests for smart contracts and wrote your first unit test.

In the next chapter, we will explore the ERC-721 token standard and how it differs from ERC-20. In addition, you'll learn to create and deploy contracts in this standard.

CHAPTER 5

ERC-721 Nonfungible Tokens

A nonfungible token (NFT) is a digital asset that represents physical objects such as art, music, in-game items, and videos. In this chapter, I'll show you how to create an NFT ERC-721 and deploy it to the Ethereum testnet network, as well as how to add it to your MetaMask mobile wallet.

At the end of this chapter, you will be able to do the following:

- Create a new NFT project

- Configure the network to deploy on Ganache

- Configure the private key

- Create the badge image

- Add the badge to the local IPFS

- Pin the badge to a remote IPFS

- Create the badge metadata

- Deploy the smart contract

- Award the badge to your wallet

- Check the badge on Etherscan

- Add the badge to your mobile wallet

© Davi Pedro Bauer 2022
D. P. Bauer, *Getting Started with Ethereum*, https://doi.org/10.1007/978-1-4842-8045-4_5

Create Your Art NFT Using Ganache and OpenZeppelin

Let's configure your first NFT using the OpenZeppelin library and create the metadata that will store the token information and then deploy it to a test network. Finally, you will view the token in your wallet.

Creating the Project

Create a new project using Truffle.

```
$ truffle init
```

Install the OpenZeppelin contracts.

```
$ npm install @openzeppelin/contracts
```

Create a new Solidity smart contract.

```
$ touch contracts/UniqueAsset.sol
```

Open the UniqueAsset.sol file and import the ERC721URIStorage.sol extension and Counters.sol utility. Create a new class extending ERC721URIStorage. Declare the counters variable and declare the constructor passing the coin name and the code.

Create a new method named awardItem. Inside the new method, increment the token ID. Get the new token number using _tokenIds. current().

Mint a new item using the method _mint. Finally, set the token URI passing the metadata using the method _setTokenURI.

```
// SPDX-License-Identifier: MIT
pragma solidity ^0.8.0;

import "@openzeppelin/contracts/token/ERC721/extensions/
ERC721URIStorage.sol";
import "@openzeppelin/contracts/utils/Counters.sol";
```

```
contract UniqueAsset is ERC721URIStorage {
    using Counters for Counters.Counter;
    Counters.Counter private _tokenIds;

    constructor() ERC721("UniqueAsset", "UNA") {}

    function awardItem(address recipient, string memory metadata)
    public
    returns (uint256)
    {
        _tokenIds.increment();
        uint256 newItemId = _tokenIds.current();
        _mint(recipient, newItemId);
        _setTokenURI(newItemId, metadata);
        return newItemId;

    }
}
```

Create a new migration file using the touch command. This command creates a new file in the migrations folder.

```
$ touch migrations/2_deploy_contracts.sol
```

Inside the 2_deploy_contracts.js file, export the smart contract in the migration file.

```
const UniqueAsset = artifacts.require("UniqueAsset");

module.exports = function (deployer) {
    deployer.deploy(UniqueAsset);
}
```

Configuring the Wallet to Sign Transactions

Install the file system fs package.

```
$ npm install fs
```

Install the wallet provider hdwallet package.

```
$ npm install @truffle/hdwallet-provider@1.2.3
```

Open the truffle-config.js file and uncomment the
HDWalletProvider code section.

```
const HDWalletProvider = require('@truffle/hdwallet-provider');
const infuraKey = '<your_infura_key>';

const fs = require('fs');
const mnemonic = fs.readFileSync(".secret").toString().trim();
```

Paste your Infura project ID as a value for the variable infuraKey.

Configuring the Network

Inside the truffle-config.js file, uncomment the ropsten network
section and make the following changes:

- – Change ropsten to rinkeby.

- – Change the Ropsten Infura URL to rinkeby.

- – Change YOU-PROJECT-ID to ${infuraKey}.

- – Change network_id to 42.

```
rinkeby: {
    provider: () => new HDWalletProvider(mnemonic, `https://
    rinkeby.infura.io/v3/${infuraKey}`),
    network_id: 42,
    gas: 5500000,
```

```
    confirmations: 2,
    timeoutBlocks: 200,
    skipDryRun: true
},
```

Configuring the Solidity Compiler

Also, inside the `truffle-config.js` file, uncomment the `compilers` section and change the version to 0.8.0.

```
compilers: {
    solc: {
        version: "0.8.0",
        docker: true,
        settings: {
            optimizer: {
                enabled: false,
                runs: 200
            },
            evmVersion: "byzantium"
        }
    }
},
```

Configuring the Private Key

Go to your browser and open your MetaMask wallet connected to the Infura network. Click "*your account*" and then click "settings." Finally, click "security & privacy" (Figure 5-1).

You have the option to view your seed phrase, but be aware that this information is sensitive, and if someone has access to it, they will be able to restore your wallet and make use of your funds.

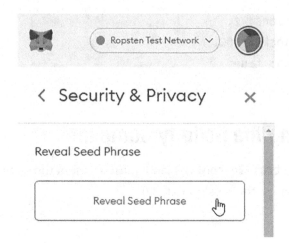

Figure 5-1. *MetaMask: revealing the seed phrase*

Click Reveal Seed Phrase and enter your wallet password to continue. Copy the private key.

Go back to Visual Studio Code and create a new file named `.secret`. Paste the private secret recovery phrase on this file.

Creating the Badge Image

Create the badge folder.

```
$ mkdir badge
```

Now, go to the badge root folder.

```
$ cd badge
```

Download the image that you will use as a badge from the Internet. You can also copy and paste an existing image into this folder. The `curl` command is used for transferring data via URL syntax.

```
$ curl https://planouhost.z15.web.core.windows.net/badge.png >
badge-image.png
```

Adding the Badge to Your Local IPFS

Initialize your local IPFS node. This command will start an IPFS local server on 127.0.0.1:5001.

```
$ ipfs daemon
```

Add your badge image to IPFS.

```
$ ipfs add badge-image.png
```

Running this command, you will receive a hash. This hash is your image address in IPFS. Make sure that you see the output shown in Figure 5-2.

```
$ ipfs add badge-image.png
 20.68 KiB / 20.68 KiB [===========================================
added QmZPxKJWqJTdudyaZUyf6uBzwwAT41QQyxhTHmMZWB9yx4 badge-image.png
 20.68 KiB / 20.68 KiB [===========================================
```

Figure 5-2. *IPFS output after adding a file*

Pinning the Badge to a Remote IPFS Node

Pin your badge using Pinata as a remote IPFS service.

```
ipfs pin remote add --service=pinata --name=badge-image.png
QmZPxKJWqJTdudyaZUyf6uBzwwAT41QQyxhTHmMZWB9yx4
```

You will get a response indicating the file was pinned successfully.

```
CID: QmZPxKJWqJTdudyaZUyf6uBzwwAT41QQyxhTHmMZWB9yx4
Name: badge-image.png
Status: pinned
```

Creating the Badge Metadata

Create the badge metadata JSON file.

```
touch badge-metadata.json
```

Open the file `badge-metadata.json` and set the badge name, description, and image address. For the last one, you can use an IPFS gateway for the image to be displayed on any wallet that supports this badge type; otherwise, you will depend on the destination wallet support displaying images from IPFS hashes directly.

```
{
    "name": "My badge",
    "description": "My badge description",
    "image": "https://ipfs.io/ipfs/QmZPxKJWqJTdudyaZUyf6uBzww
    AT41QQyxhTHmMZWB9yx4"
}
```

Add your badge metadata to IPFS.

```
$ ipfs add badge-metadata.json
```

Pin your badge metadata using a remote IPFS service.

```
$ ipfs pin remote add --service=pinata --name=badge-metadata.
json QmRzcwAtLWbeYqyaZUyf6uBzwwAT41QQyxhTHmMZWBfUTa
```

Compiling the Smart Contract

Compile the contract using Truffle.

```
$ truffle compile
```

Migrating the Smart Contract

Migrate the contract to the Rinkeby network using Truffle.

```
$ truffle migrate --network rinkeby
```

Instantiate the Smart Contract

Instantiate the contract using the Truffle console.

```
$ truffle console --network rinkeby
```

Get the instance of the deployed contract.

```
truffle(rinkeby) let instance = await UniqueAsset.deployed()
```

Awarding a Badge to a Wallet

Call the method awardItem and pass the Ethereum address as a first parameter and the IPFS address for the badge metadata. Make sure that the IPFS address corresponds to your badge metadata.

```
truffle(rinkeby) let result = await instance.awardItem
("0x62761466bB3A3Da83B408B5F5fE00ac7b2a5A996","https://ipfs.io/
ipfs/QmRzcwAtLWBeYqUx3ba1BkYKubSDLNTHCuiUB7WAmdfUTa")
```

Checking a Badge on Etherscan

Once your contract is deployed, you will be able to see the public address of your contract. Find in the terminal the contract address created and copy it.

Go to `https://rinkeby.etherscan.io` and paste the contract address in the search bar (Figure 5-3). You can use the Rinkeby Testnet Explorer tool to view the details of the created smart contract.

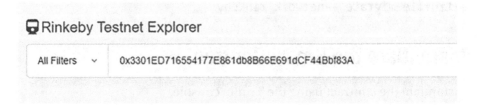

Figure 5-3. *Rinkeby Testnet Explorer: searching for a smart contract*

Click the search icon. Now you can see that the contract was deployed successfully (Figure 5-4). On this details page, you can view data such as transactions.

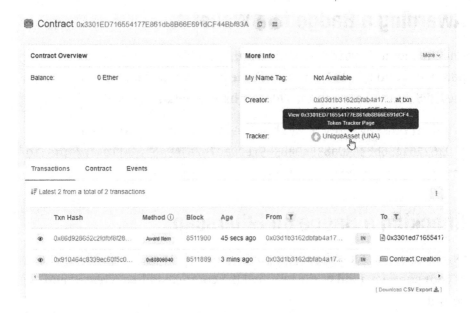

Figure 5-4. *Rinkeby Testnet Explorer: viewing smart contract transactions*

You can also realize that the last transaction made was for awarding a new item.

Adding the NFT Token to Your Wallet

Open your MetaMask wallet on your mobile phone and click Collectibles (Figure 5-5). Notice that the collectibles are available only on a mobile version.

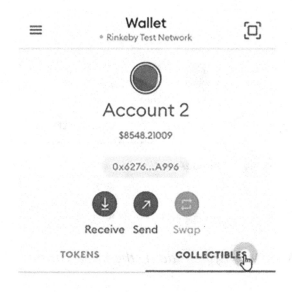

Figure 5-5. *MetaMask: Collectibles tab*

Click Add Collectibles. Paste the token contract address here (the same one that you copied in the previous section) and enter the token ID (as it is the first token you will enter a 1 here).

Click Add and wait for a few seconds (Figure 5-6). The NFT token was added!

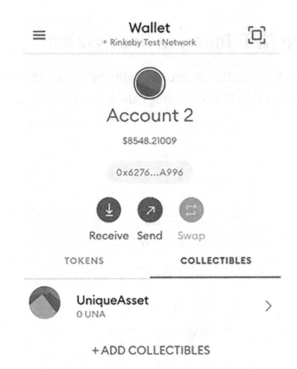

Figure 5-6. *MetaMask: after adding the smart contract, it will appear here*

Click UniqueAsset. Now you will be able to see all the badges that you earn (Figure 5-7). You can have multiple tokens originating from the same smart contract, each of which will be distinguished by a unique identifier.

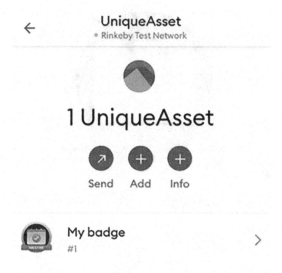

Figure 5-7. *MetaMask: badge listing*

Click "My badge." Now you can see the badge details! Also, you have a Send button so that you can send the badge to another wallet (Figure 5-8).

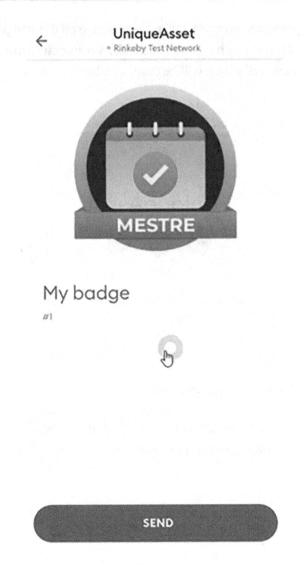

Figure 5-8. MetaMask: badge display

That's it! You just created your first NFT token!

Sell Your Art NFT on OpenSea

OpenSea is a marketplace for digital goods such as collectibles, gaming items, digital art, and other digital assets backed by a blockchain such as Ethereum. You can purchase, sell, and trade any of these things with anyone in the world on OpenSea.

Connecting to OpenSea

Go to OpenSea[1] and make sure that you are connected to the wallet that contains the NFT and that you are using the Rinkeby test network.

Viewing Your Badge

Go to My Profile. Click Activity and then click the badge title. These are your badge details. The details page allows you to view various information regarding the negotiation of your badge.

Listing Your Badge for Sale

Click Sell and then click Set Price. In Price, set the price that you desire to sell the NFT. On this page you can set the badge pricing method as well as schedule it to be listed at a future date (Figure 5-9).

---

[1]https://testnets.opensea.io

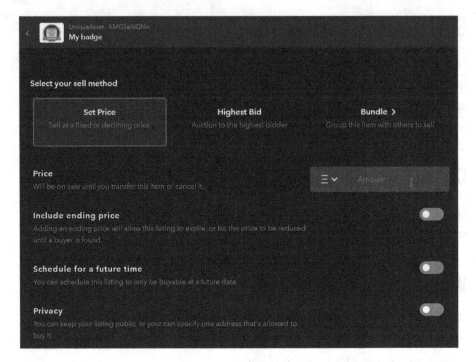

Figure 5-9. *OpenSea: badge pricing page*

Click Post Your Listing. You will be redirected to the Summary page (Figure 5-10). On this page you can see the total fees that will be deducted when selling your badge.

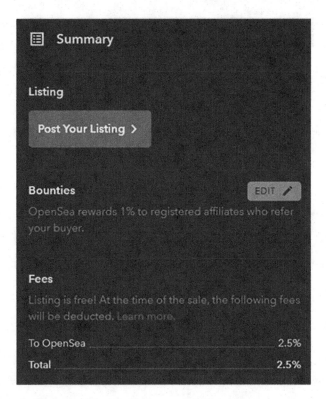

Figure 5-10. *OpenSea: badge's Summary page*

MetaMask will be open in order to validate the transaction
(Figure 5-11). Click Confirm. In this step you need to approve the
transaction that will confirm the listing of your badge for sale on the
platform.

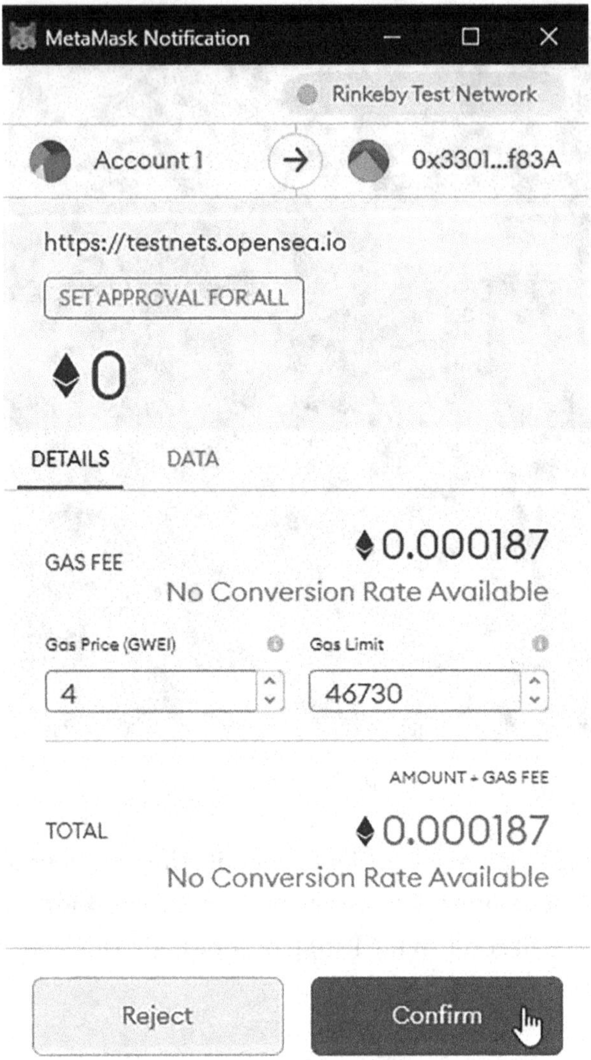

Figure 5-11. *MetaMask: confirm OpenSea transaction*

Now you will need to provide some more details about you, such as your email and nickname. You will be asked to provide additional information after the transaction is approved (Figure 5-12).

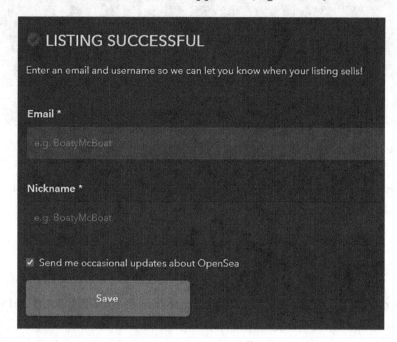

Figure 5-12. *OpenSea: additional information*

Click Save. Now, OpenSea will list your NFT for you!

Exploring Listing Details

Scroll down to Trading History (Figure 5-13); as you can see, a new event was created named List and with Price set at US 10. On this page you can see all the badge trading history on the platform.

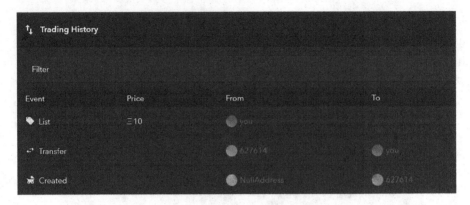

Figure 5-13. *OpenSea: trading history*

Click the Share icon. You can copy the link or share it on your social networks.

Summary

In this chapter, you learned how to create tokens in the ERC-721 standard, pin the image in IPFS, and import it in OpenSea and put it up for sale.

In the next chapter, we will find out how to use faucets and why they are important in testnets.

CHAPTER 6

Faucets

You can use faucets to test smart contracts on the test network with no need to use real ether for this purpose (because ether from the mainnet is not valid in testnets, and vice versa). Ether in a test network has no real value except for testing purposes in smart contracts development.

At the end of this chapter, you will be able to do the following:

- Access the faucet on the Ropsten network

- Access the faucet on the Rinkeby network

- Access the faucet on the Polygon Mumbai test network

- Access the faucet on the Polygon main network

- Send test ether to your wallet

- Send test MATIC to your wallet

- Check the updated balance in your wallet

Getting Test Ether from the Faucet on the Ropsten Network

This Ethereum test faucet[1] drips 1 ether every five seconds. You have a request limit of 1 eth for every 24 hours to avoid network spam.

---

[1] `https://faucet.ropsten.be`

© Davi Pedro Bauer 2022
D. P. Bauer, *Getting Started with Ethereum*, https://doi.org/10.1007/978-1-4842-8045-4_6

Accessing the Faucet

Go to the Ropsten Ethereum (rETH) Faucet[2] and copy your wallet address (make sure the network selected is Ropsten). Paste your contract address in the form field. Click "Send Ropsten ETH", as shown in Figure 6-1.

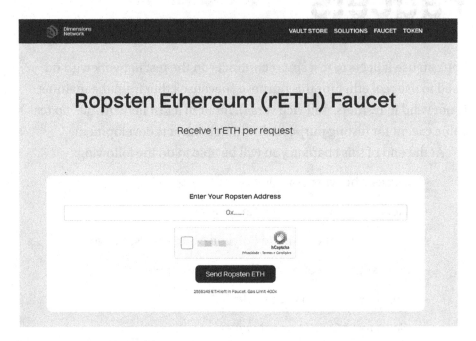

Figure 6-1. *Ropsten faucet home page*

Waiting for the Transaction

Click the transaction hash (which opens a new window) and wait for the transaction to be completed. Once the transaction has successfully completed, go to your MetaMask wallet, and you will see that you now have 1 ether!

---

[2] https://faucet.dimensions.network/

Getting Test Ether from the Faucet on the Rinkeby Testnet

This ether faucet is connected to the Rinkeby network. Requests are tied to common third-party social network accounts to prevent malicious actors from exhausting all the available funds or accumulating enough ether to mount long-running spam attacks. Anyone with a Twitter or Facebook account may request funds up to the allowed limits.

Preparing for Funding

Open your MetaMask wallet and copy your wallet address to clipboard. Go to your Twitter account and paste in your wallet address. Click your tweet and copy your tweet address (the URL in the address bar).

Funding Your Wallet

Go to `https://faucet.rinkeby.io` and paste your tweet address in the text field, as shown in Figure 6-2. Click "Give me Ether" and select one of the options available (for example, 3 Ethers / 8 hours). The request will be funded in a few seconds.

It is important to note that there are varieties of faucets available. Periodically some of them may be empty, or over time they may run out of activity. Or, new faucets may even be created. If any of them become unavailable, you can search for new ones on the Internet.

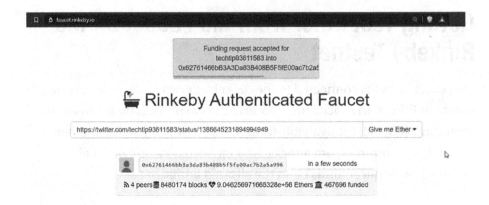

Figure 6-2. *Rinkeby faucet home page*

Checking Your Wallet

Wait a few moments and check your MetaMask wallet. You will get 3 ether in your wallet account!

Getting Test MATIC from the Faucet on the Mumbai Testnet

This faucet transfers TestToken/MATIC-ETH on Matic testnets and the corresponding parent chain.

Preparing for Funding

Open your MetaMask wallet and copy your wallet address to the clipboard.

Funding Your Wallet

Go to `https://faucet.matic.network`. For the token, select MATIC Token, and for the network, select Mumbai. Paste your tweet address in the text field and click Submit (Figure 6-3). The confirmation details will be provided for you. Click Confirm. The request will be funded in a few seconds.

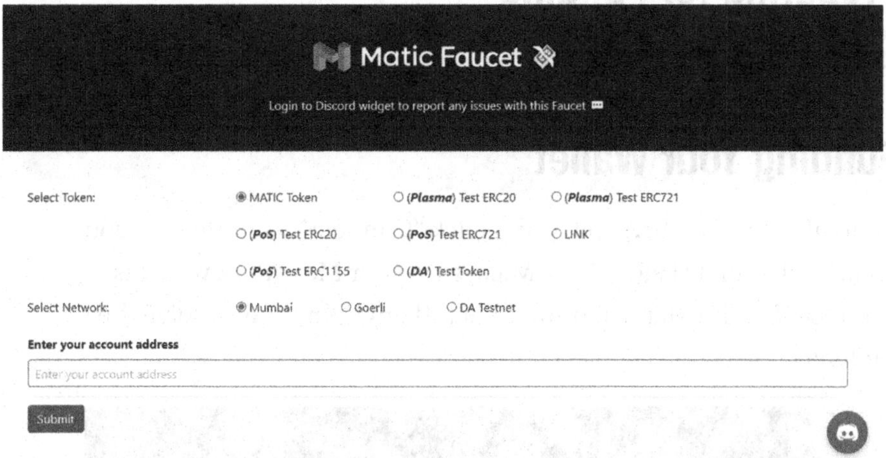

Figure 6-3. *Matic faucet home page*

Checking Your Wallet

Wait a few moments and check your MetaMask wallet. You will get 0.1 MATIC in your wallet account!

Getting the Test MATIC from the Faucet on the Mainnet

This faucet transfers TestToken/MATIC-ETH on Polygon testnets and the corresponding parent chain.

Preparing for Funding

Open your MetaMask wallet and copy your wallet address to the clipboard.

Funding Your Wallet

Go to `https://matic.supply` and click "Connect" to connect to your MetaMask wallet (Figure 6-4). Make sure your MetaMask wallet is connected to the Matic mainnet. Click "I am human" and solve the captcha.

Figure 6-4. Polygon faucet home page

Checking Your Wallet

Wait a few moments and check your MetaMask wallet. You have just received 0.001 MATIC in your wallet!

Summary

In this chapter, you learned how to get test ether from faucets on the Internet. This will be very useful for deploying contracts on test networks so you don't have to spend real ether.

CHAPTER 7

InterPlanetary File System

The InterPlanetary File System[1] (IPFS) is a protocol and peer-to-peer network that allows data to be stored and shared in a distributed file system. IPFS employs content addressing to distinguish each file in a global namespace that connects all computing devices.

At the end of this chapter, you will be able to do the following:

- Install the IPFS node package and initialize a node

- View the IPFS node peers

- Test and explore the IPFS node

- Add files to IPFS

- View the file content on the console and check the file in the web UI

- View the file content directly in a browser

- Install the IPFS browser extension

- Configure the IPFS node type and start a node

- Import a file into the IPFS node

---

[1] https://ipfs.io

D. P. Bauer, *Getting Started with Ethereum*, https://doi.org/10.1007/978-1-4842-8045-4_7

- Start a local IPFS node and add files to it

- Check the files added and verify whether a file has been pinned

- Pin the files manually

- Set up API keys on Pinata

- Set up Pinata as a remote service

- Pin your file to the remote IPFS node and also unpin it

- Log in to Fleek

- Clone an existing repository

- Install and initialize the Fleek package

- Deploy a site to Fleek

Create Your IPFS Node

Now, let's create an IPFS node using the command line and upload your first file.

Installing the Node

Install the IPFS using the Choco package manager.[2] The package go-ipfs is an IPFS implementation in Go.

```
$ choco install go-ipfs
```

---

[2] https://chocolatey.org

Configuring the Node

Initiate the IPFS local repository.

```
$ ipfs init
```

Start the IPFS local server. The daemon command starts an IPFS local server on 127.0.0.1:5001.

```
$ ipfs daemon
```

Testing the Node

You can test the IPFS node showing the peers that are directly connected to your node.

```
$ ipfs swarm peers
```

You can also view some IPFS file content by using the cat command and passing the hash as a parameter (Figure 7-1).

```
$ ipfs cat <hash>
```

Figure 7-1. *IPFS cat command output*

Exploring Your IPFS Node

Go to a browser and access the web UI at http://127.0.0.1:5002/. Your node is now connected to IPFS! Now, click Files and notice that are no files here yet (Figure 7-2).

Click "Explore" and then click "Peers". These are the peers that you are connected to. Finally, click "Settings". This is where you can see your node settings.

Figure 7-2. *IPFS Web UI*

Add Files to the IPFS

A computer running IPFS can ask all the peers to which it is connected
if they have a file with a specific hash, and if one of them does, that peer
sends back the entire file. That would not be possible without a short,
unique identifier, such as a cryptographic hash.

Adding the File

Start the IPFS local server. The daemon command starts an IPFS local server
on 127.0.0.1:5001.

```
$ ipfs daemon
```

Now, create a new file called hello.txt using the echo command. This
command outputs the given text to a new file.

```
$ echo "test" hello.txt
```

Add the newly created file to your local IPFS node using the `ipfs add` command.

```
$ ipfs add hello.txt
```

The file was added to IPFS, resulting in a hash identifier.

Viewing the File Content on the Console

You can see the file content of this newly added file simply using the `ipfs cat` command followed by the hash. For that, replace the *<your_hash>* code snipped by the result hash identifier generated in the previous step by the command "`ipfs add hello.txt`".

```
$ ipfs cat <your_hash>
```

After running this command, the file content will be displayed on the terminal.

Checking the File in the Web UI

Got to `http://127.0.0.1:5001/webui` and click "Files". Now, click "Pins" and copy the hash. Search by using this hash, and you will see that this hash is there.

Viewing the File Content in a Browser

Open a new tab and go to `ipfs://<your_hash>`. Now you can see your file content in the browser. Here again, replace the *<your_hash>* code snipped by the result hash identifier generated for your file with the command "`ipfs cat <your_hash>`".

Set Up the IPFS Browser Extension

The IPFS Companion Extension[3] allows you to run an IPFS node locally inside your preferred browser, providing support for `ipfs://` addresses, automatic IPFS gateway loading of websites and file paths, simple IPFS file import and sharing, and more.

Installing the Browser Extension

Go to the IPFS Companion Extension[4] and click "Add to Brave" or the name of your browser. Click "Add extension" and then click the "Extensions" icon. Finally, pin the IPFS Companion Extension to the extensions bar.

Configuring the Node Type

Click the IPFS Companion icon and then click the gear icon. For IPFS Node Type, select External.

Starting an External Node

Go to Visual Studio Code and open a new terminal. Start a new IPFS local server.

```
$ ipfs daemon
```

---

[3] https://chrome.google.com/webstore/detail/ipfs-companion/nibjojkom
fdiaoajekhjakgkdhaomnch

[4] https://chrome.google.com/webstore/detail/ipfs-companion/nibjojkomfdi
aoajekhjakgkdhaomnch?hl=en

Importing a File

Click the IPFS Companion icon and then click "Import". Click "Pick a file" and select a file from your local disc. The file will be stored in your IPFS node.

Pin and Unpin IPFS Files on the Local Node

Data can be pinned to one or more IPFS nodes to ensure that it remains on IPFS and is not removed during garbage collection. Pinning allows you to manage storage space and data retention. Therefore, you should go ahead pin any content that you want to keep on IPFS indefinitely. IPFS's default behavior is to pin files to your local IPFS node.

Starting Your Local Node

Start the IPFS local server. The daemon command starts an IPFS local server on 127.0.0.1:5001.

```
$ ipfs daemon
```

Adding a File to Your Node

Now, create a new file called hello.txt using the echo command. This command outputs the given text to a new file.

```
$ echo "world" hello.txt
```

Add the newly created file to your local IPFS node using the ipfs add command.

```
$ ipfs add hello.txt
```

The file was added to IPFS, resulting in a hash identifier. When you add a file, this is automatically pinned to your local node.

Checking the File Was Added

To check that your file was added, you can use the `ipfs cat` command to output the file content to the terminal.

```
$ ipfs cat your_file_hash
```

Verifying Your File Was Pinned

Go to `http://127.0.0.1:5001/webui`, click Files, and then click Pins. Your file is there!

Unpinning Your File

You can unpin the file from your local IPFS node simply by using the following command:

```
$ ipfs pin rm <your_file_hash>
```

Pinning Your File Manually

You can pin files manually using the following command. Remember that you need to copy the hash of your file to pin or unpin it.

```
$ ipfs pin add <your_file_hash>
```

You're done; your file was pinned again!

Pin and Unpin Files on a Remote Node Using Pinata

You can also pin your files to a remote pinning service. These third-party services allow you to pin files to nodes that they operate rather than your own local node. You don't have to be concerned about your own node's disk space or uptime.

While you can manage IPFS files pinned to a remote pinning service using its own GUI, CLI, or other dev tools, you can also work directly with pinning services using your local IPFS installation, eliminating the need to learn a pinning service's unique API or other tooling.

Setting Up API Keys on Pinata

Log in on your Pinata account and go to API Keys. Click New Key and then check the Admin box. Enter **admin-cli** as your key name and finally click Create Key. A new key will be generated for you. Copy the JWT value from this window.

Setting Up Pinata as a Remote Service on Your Terminal

Add Pinata as a pinning remote service. Paste your JWT inside the *<your_jwt_key>* chunk.

```
$ ipfs pin remote service add pinata https://api.pinata.cloud/
psa <your_jwt_key>
```

List all the existing remote services and check that Pinata is there.

```
$ ipfs pin remote service ls
```

Adding a New File to Your Local IPFS Node

Add a new file to your IPFS local node.

```
$ echo "world" > hello.txt
$ ipfs add hello.txt
```

Copy the hash identifier generated after adding the file to the local node.

Pinning Your File to the Remote IPFS Node

Pin your file using the following command. Paste the file hash inside the *<your_file_hash>* chunk.

```
$ ipfs pin remote add --service=pinata -name=hello.txt <your_
file_hash>
```

Go back to the Pinata website and click Pin Manager. Your file will appear on this page!

Unpinning Your File from the Remote IPFS Node

Unpin your file using the following command. Paste the file hash inside your *<your_file_hash>* chunk.

```
$ ipfs pin remote rm --service=pinata -name=hello.txt <your_
file_hash>
```

Go back to the Pinata website and click Pin Manager. Your file will no longer appear on this page; that means your file was unpinned.

Host Your Site on IPFS Using Fleek

Fleek enables you to create a base-layer architecture based on Open Web protocols. Create and host your sites, apps, DApps, and other services on trustless, permissionless, and open technologies that are geared toward enabling user-controlled, encrypted, private, peer-to-peer experiences.

Logging In on Fleek

Go to `https://fleek.co` and log in with your account; then go to your VS Code editor.

Cloning Your Existing Repository

Clone an existing repository with some sample code.

```
$ git clone https://github.com/johnnymatthews/random-
planet-facts
```

Installing Fleek

Install the Fleek command line.

```
$ npm install -g @fleekhq/fleek-cli
```

Log in to your Fleek account (you will be prompted to complete the flow in your browser).

```
$ fleek login
```

Initializing Fleek

Initialize the Fleek site in your current directory.

```
$ fleek site:init
```

You will be asked to select which team you want to use (use the arrow keys for selecting). Also, select which site you want to use. Finally, select the public directory for deployment.

Deploying Your Site

Deploy the changes in your `publish` directory.

```
$ fleek site:deploy
```

Go back to the Fleek site and click Hosting; then click Verify on IPFS. This is your site hosted on IPFS. You can now see your deployed site online.

Go back to Hosting and click `your-site.on.fleek.co`. This is your site host's friendly address (Figure 7-3).

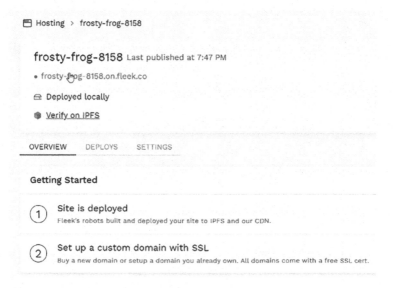

Figure 7-3. *Fleek hosting overview*

Summary

In this chapter, you learned how to install and create an IPFS node, as well as manage files with this protocol.

In the next chapter, you will learn how to create a Filecoin project.

CHAPTER 8

Filecoin

Protocol Labs, the same company that invented and maintains IPFS, created Filecoin. It expands the IPFS concept by establishing an open source decentralized storage network and incentivizes users to keep data pinned to IPFS.

Filecoin is great because it offers a decentralized storage solution that does not require reliance on bigger centralized storage solutions. Unlike pure IPFS-based solutions, Filecoin nodes have financial incentives to stay active.

We will use a Filecoin implementation named Lotus in this example. It verifies network transactions, manages an FIL wallet, and can execute storage and retrieval deals.

At the end of this chapter, you will be able to do the following:

- Create a Filecoin project

- Configure Truffle to use Filecoin endpoints

- Start the local Filecoin server

- Add images to be preserved on Filecoin

© Davi Pedro Bauer 2022

D. P. Bauer, *Getting Started with Ethereum*, https://doi.org/10.1007/978-1-4842-8045-4_8

How to Preserve Files on the Filecoin Local Node

To preserve files in Filecoin, you will learn how to create a project from scratch and configure Truffle so that it points to the correct address. You will start the local endpoints and finally add an image to Filecoin using the command line.

Creating the Project

Go to the terminal and click New Terminal. Now, create a new folder to start your project.

```
$ mkdir create filecoin
```

Configuring Truffle

Create the truffle-config.js file.

```
$ touch truffle-config.js
```

In this file, configure the file setting for the IPFS and Filecoin lotus servers. Set the following values:

- Set the IPFS address to http://127.0.0.1:5001.

- Set the Filecoin address to http://localhost:7777/rpc/v0.

You will use Ganache Filecoin to start these endpoints later.

```
module.exports = {
  environments: {
    development: {
      ipfs: {
        address: "http://127.0.0.1:5001",
      },
```

```
    filecoin: {
      address: "http://localhost:7777/rpc/v0",
      storageDealOptions: {
        epochPrice: "2500",
        duration: 518400,
      }
    },
  }
}
};
```

Adding an Image to Be Preserved

Create the badge folder.

```
$ mkdir badge
```

Go to the badge root folder.

```
$ cd badge
```

Download the image that you will use to preserve on Filecoin. You can also copy and paste an existing image in this folder. The `curl` command is used for transferring data with a URL syntax.

```
$ curl https://planouhost.z15.web.core.windows.net/badge.png >
badge-image.png
```

Installing Dependencies

Install the base Ganache package with a Filecoin tag.

```
$ npm install ganache@filecoin
```

Install the Filecoin peer dependency package.

```
$ npm install @ganache/filecoin
```

Start the Lotus and IPFS local servers using Ganache. It also creates 10 development accounts with 100 Filecoins (FIL) each.

Starting Local Endpoints

Start Ganache Filecoin locally.

```
$ npx ganache filecoin
```

Preserving Files to Filecoin

Open a new terminal and preserve the folder badge.

```
$ truffle preserve ./badge/ --filecoin
```

If everything went well, the output will be as follows:

```
Preserving target: ./badge/
============================
Warning: multiple plugins found that output the label "ipfs-cid".

 ✓ Loading target...
   ✓ Reading directory ./badge/...
     ✓ Opening ./badge\badge-image.png...

 ✓ Preserving to IPFS...
   ✓ Connected to IPFS node at http://127.0.0.1:5001
   ✓ Uploading...
     Root CID: QmNjGGACAMpm718WjeM7oN3WJ5ntXKgwurH4mMivU6JXoS
       ./badge-image.png: QmemrBxhPpg8Hw9sPpAUTWRq3kNAFhCPKUD
       hMnc5U9KptS
```

```
✓ Preserving to Filecoin...
  ✓ Connected to Filecoin node at http://localhost:7777/rpc/v0
  ✓ Retrieving miners...
  ✓ Proposing storage deal...
    Deal CID: bafyreidrt2pvuh44umo7vzebnxnw46qzntneyojah6oym4
    ximokyzvwxgq
  ✓ Waiting for deal to finish...
    Deal State: StorageDealActive
```

Now you have the image preserved in your local Filecoin node!

Summary

In this chapter, you learned how to preserve files using Filecoin.

In the next chapter, you will learn what ENS is and how to use it.

CHAPTER 9

Ethereum Name Service

The Ethereum Name Service (ENS) allows users to send and receive Ethereum as well as access special websites by using simple names rather than long, complex sequences of letters and numbers.

At the end of this chapter, you will be able to do the following:

- Search for a domain name on the ENS network

- Register an available domain

- Manage an ENS registration name

- Check an ENS name resolution

Register Your ENS to Receive Crypto, Tokens, or NFTs in Your Wallet

Let's search for an available domain name in ENS and register it. Next, you will manage the address through a registration page. Finally, you'll check if the domain is resolving correctly to the address that is configured.

Searching for Your Domain Name

Go to the ENS Domains[1] page and click Launch App. Search for the domain name that you want to register (for example, `planou.eth`). Check the registration period (for example, a minimum of one year) and the registration price.

Registering Your Name

Click Request to Register. A MetaMask notification will open to confirm the transaction. Click Confirm and wait for the transaction to be confirmed on the blockchain. Once it's confirmed, click Register. A new MetaMask notification will appear. Click Confirm once again and wait for the transaction to be confirmed on the blockchain.

Managing Your Registration Name

Click "Manage name" and scroll down to Addresses. Realize that the ETH address is set to the wallet that created the domain, in this case, your wallet (Figure 9-1).

---

[1] `https://ens.domains`

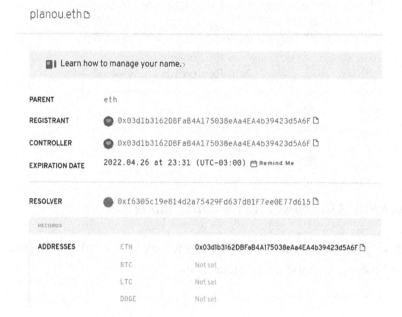

Figure 9-1. *ENS domain registration page*

Checking the Name Resolution

Click your MetaMask wallet and click Send. Type your ENS name (for example, `planou.eth`). Note that the name has resolved to a wallet address (Figure 9-2).

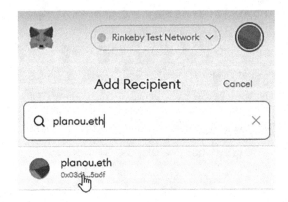

Figure 9-2. *MetaMask ENS resolution name*

Now you can use the ENS name as a recipient instead of using the wallet hash address for your transactions.

Summary

In this chapter, you learned how simple configuring an ENS domain is, and you learned how to start using it right away.

In the next chapter, you will start learning about how to get off-chain data with oracles using Chainlink.

CHAPTER 10

Chainlink

Chainlink[1] is a decentralized network of nodes that uses oracles to transfer data and information from off-blockchain sources to on-blockchain smart contracts. In this chapter, you will learn how to use the ETH/USD price feed on the Kovan testnet to access the most recent cryptocurrency price inside smart contracts.

At the end of this chapter, you will be able to do the following:

- Create a simple smart contact for price consumption

- Set up an Infura project

- Configure the private key to sign transactions

- Deploy the smart contract on the Kovan network

- Get price information from the smart contact on the Kovan network

---

[1] https://chain.link

© Davi Pedro Bauer 2022
D. P. Bauer, *Getting Started with Ethereum*, https://doi.org/10.1007/978-1-4842-8045-4_10

Get Crypto Prices Inside Smart Contracts Using Chainlink Oracles

Let's start by creating a new project and then installing the Chainlink contracts package. You will use an existing contract address that tells you the price of the ETH/USD pair, and then you will be able to see that price being returned by your smart contact.

Creating the Project

Go to the Terminal menu, click New Terminal, and initialize a new Truffle project.

```
$ truffle init
```

Now, initialize the project folder.

```
$ npm init
```

Finally, install the Chainlink contracts package.[2]

```
$ npm install @chainlink/contracts@0.1.9
```

Creating the Smart Contract

Create a new smart contract for price consumption.

```
$ touch contracts/PriceConsumer.sol
```

Open the file PriceConsumer.sol (Figure 10-1).

---

[2] https://www.npmjs.com/package/@chainlink/contracts

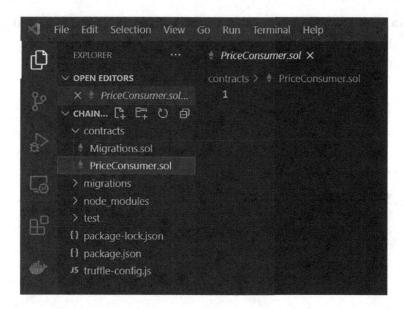

Figure 10-1. *VS Code contracts folder*

In the `PriceConsumer.sol` file, define the Solidity version and then import the Chainlink contract interface. After that, define the contract name and the contract constructor.

```
// SPDX-License-Identifier: MIT
pragma solidity ^0.8.0;

import "@chainlink/contracts/src/v0.6/interfaces/
AggregatorV3Interface.sol";

contract PriceConsumer {

    AggregatorV3Interface internal priceFeed;

    constructor(){
        priceFeed = AggregatorV3Interface()
    }
}
```

Go to `https://docs.chain.link/docs/ethereum-addresses` and scroll down to the Kovan section. Copy the Proxy address on the line "ETH/USD" (Figure 10-2).

USING PRICE FEEDS			
	BTC / USD	8	0x6135b13325bfC4B00027884abC5e20bbce2D6580e
Introduction to Price Feeds	BUSD / ETH	18	0xbF7A18ea5DE0501f7559144e702b29c55b055CcB
Get the Latest Price	BZRX / ETH	18	0x9aa9da35DC44F93D90436BfE256f465f720c3Ae5
Historical Price Data	CHF / USD	8	0xed0616BeF04D374969f302a34AE4A63882490A8C
API Reference	COMP / USD	8	0xECF93D14d25E02bA2C1369BeeDca9aA98348EFb6
Contract Addresses	CVI	18	0x0BD102ef50a6a133B38Bf3Bd3d40cE36cc1aB5A8
ENS	DAI / ETH	18	0x22B58f1EbEDfCA50feF632bD73368b2FdA96D541
Ethereum Price Feeds	DAI / USD	8	0x777A68032a88E5A84678A77Af2CD65A7b3c0775a
Binance Smart Chain Price Feeds	ENJ / ETH	18	0xfaDbe2ee798889F02d1d39eDaD98Eff4c7fe95D4
Polygon (Matic) Price Feeds	ETH / USDT RSI 4h	18	0x10900f50d1bC46b4Ed796C50A4Cc63791CaF7501
xDai Price Feeds	ETH / USD	8	0x9326BFA02ADD2366b30bacB125260Af641031331
Huobi Eco Chain Price Feeds	EUR / USD	8	0x0c15Ab9A0DB086e062194c273CC79f41597Bbf13
USING RANDOMNESS			
Introduction to Chainlink VRF	Ferrari F12 TDF / USD	8	0x22a2D07993A1A18b3b86E56F960fa735b6D6cED9
Get a Random Number			

Figure 10-2. *Chainlink price feeds*

Paste the address into the `AggregatorV3Interface` constructor. After that, create the function to get the price.

```
// SPDX-License-Identifier: MIT
pragma solidity ^0.8.0;

import "@chainlink/contracts/src/v0.6/interfaces/
AggregatorV3Interface.sol";

contract PriceConsumer {

    AggregatorV3Interface internal priceFeed;
    constructor(){
        priceFeed = AggregatorV3Interface(0x9326BFA02ADD2366b30
                    bacB125260Af641031331);
    }
```

```solidity
function getThePrice() public view returns (int){
    (
        uint80 roundID,
        int price,
        uint startedAt,
        uint timeStamp,
        uint80 answeredInRound
    ) = priceFeed.latestRoundData();
    return price;
    }
}
```

Creating the Migration

Create the migration file in the migrations folder.

```
$ touch migrations/2_deploy_contracts.sol
```

Write code to deploy the PriceConsumer smart contract (Figure 10-3).

```javascript
const PriceConsumer = artifacts.require("PriceConsumer");

module.exports = function(deployer){
    deployer.deploy(PriceConsumer);
};
```

Figure 10-3. *VS Code migrations folder*

Setting Up Your Infura Project

Go to https://infura.io and access your dashboard. Click Ethereum and then click "Create a project". Finally, define the project name and copy the project ID (Figure 10-4). Notice that you can connect with different testnets and also to the mainnet.

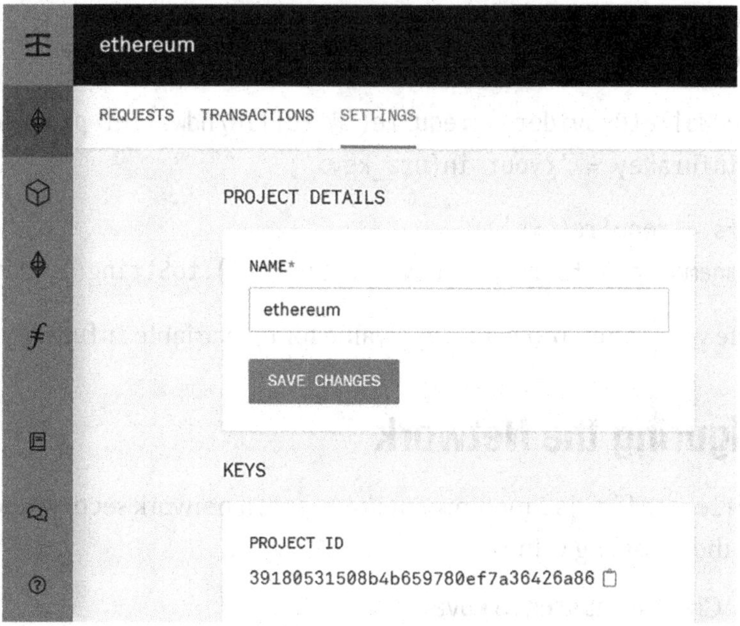

Figure 10-4. *Infura settings*

Now, click Save Changes.

Configuring the Wallet to Sign Transactions

Install the file system fs package. This package provides a lot of useful functionality to access and interact with the file system.

```
$ npm install fs
```

Install the wallet provider hdwallet package. This also installs the HD wallet-enabled Web 3 provider, which is used to sign transactions for addresses derived from a 12- or 24-word mnemonic.

```
$ npm install @truffle/hdwallet-provider@1.2.3
```

Open the truffle-config.js file and uncomment the
HDWalletProvider code section.

```
const HDWalletProvider = require('@truffle/hdwallet-provider');
const infuraKey = '<your_infura_key>';

const fs = require('fs');
const mnemonic = fs.readFileSync(".secret").toString().trim();
```

Paste your Infura project ID as a value for the variable infuraKey.

Configuring the Network

In truffle-config.js, uncomment the ropsten network section and
change the following values:

- Change ropsten to kovan.

- Change the Ropsten Infura URL to kovan.

- Change YOUR-PROJECT-ID to ${infuraKey}.

- Change network_id to 42.

```
kovan: {
    provider: () => new HDWalletProvider(mnemonic, `
    https://kovan.infura.io/v3/${infuraKey}`),
    network_id: 42,
    gas: 5500000,
    confirmations: 2,
    timeoutBlocks: 200,
    skipDryRun: true
},
```

Configuring the Solidity Compiler

Still in `truffle.config.js`, uncomment the `compilers` section and change the version to `0.8.0`.

```
compilers: {
    solc: {
        version: "0.8.0",
        docker: true,
        settings: {
            optimizer: {
                enabled: false,
                runs: 200
            },
            evmVersion: "byzantium"
        }
    }
},
```

Configuring the Private Key

Create the secret file as follows:

```
$ touch .secret
```

Go to the browser and open your MetaMask wallet connected to the Infura network. Click "Your Account" and then click "Settings". Finally, click "Security & Privacy" (Figure 10-5).

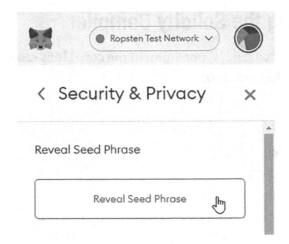

Figure 10-5. *MetaMask: revealing the seed phrase*

You have the option to view your seed phrase, but be aware that this information is sensitive, and if someone has access to it, they will be able to restore your wallet and make use of your funds.

Click Reveal Seed Phrase and enter your wallet password to continue. Copy the private key. Go back to Visual Studio Code and paste the private secret recovery phrase in the file `.secret`.

Compiling the Smart Contract

Compile the contract using Truffle.

```
$ truffle compile
```

Deploying the Smart Contract

Deploy the contract to the Kovan network using Truffle. The `migrate` command runs migrations to deploy contracts on the Kovan network.

```
$ truffle migrate --network kovan
```

Wait for the contract to be deployed and the transactions to be confirmed on the blockchain. Now, check your contract address that was created (Figure 10-6).

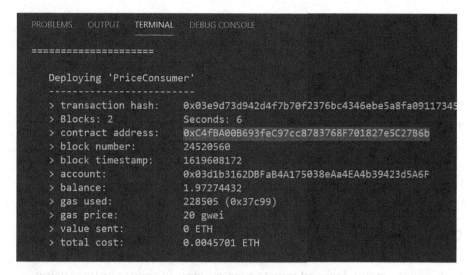

Figure 10-6. *VS Code deployed contract output*

Getting the Price Information from the Smart Contract

Instantiate the contract using the Truffle console. This console command opens a basic interactive console that connects to an Ethereum client on the Kovan network:

```
$ truffle console --network kovan
```

Now, use the deployed command to return the deployed contract instance on the Kovan network, as shown here:

```
truffle(kovan) let instance = await PriceConsumer.deployed()
```

Call the method getThePrice. The let command stores the method result in the variable price, and the await command will execute the method asynchronously.

```
truffle(kovan) let price = await instance.getThePrice()
```

Finally, output the result to number. The method toNumber() converts big number objects to regular numbers.

```
truffle(kovan) price.toNumber()
265499339990
```

That's it, you just created a smart contract and consumed the Chainlink price feed oracle!

Summary

In this chapter, you learned how to create a simple smart contract using Chainlink to get price information from a Chainlink oracle.

In the next chapter, you will learn about Nethereum, a .NET library for Ethereum.

CHAPTER 11

Nethereum

Nethereum[1] is an open source .NET integration library for Ethereum that simplifies smart contract maintenance and interaction with public and private Ethereum nodes. This framework exposes a `Web3` class where it is possible to interact with methods of wallets or smart contracts. In the example that you will see in this chapter, you will use the `GetBalance` method of a wallet to find out its balance.

At the end of this chapter, you will be able to do the following:

- Create a new console project using dotnet

- Create a method to get a wallet balance using Nethereum

- Display the result in the console

Getting Your Ether Balance Using Nethereum

Let's start by creating a new console project and adding the Nethereum `Web3` package to our application. Then you will create the method that will fetch the balance of a specific wallet address. Finally, you will print this information to the console in wei and in ether.

---

[1] `https://nethereum.com`

© Davi Pedro Bauer 2022
D. P. Bauer, *Getting Started with Ethereum*, https://doi.org/10.1007/978-1-4842-8045-4_11

Creating the Project

Go to the terminal and click New Terminal. Create a new dotnet console project as follows. This command creates a new project, configuration file, or solution based on the specified template:

```
$ dotnet new console -o sample
```

Go to the project's root directory.

```
$ cd sample
```

Installing Web3

Install the Nethereum Web3 package. This command adds a package reference to a project file:

```
$ dotnet add package Nethereum.Web3
```

Restore all the project packages. This command restores the dependencies and tools of a project:

```
$ dotnet restore
```

Creating the Method

Open the Program.cs file and add a reference for threading and Web3. Now, add a new method for getting the account balance and then instantiate a new Web3 object.

Go to your Infura project settings and select the Ropsten network. Copy the Ropsten https endpoint (Figure 11-1).

120

KEYS

PROJECT ID   PROJECT SECRET

39180531508b4b659780ef7a36426a86 🗐

ENDPOINTS | Ropsten | ∨ |

https://ropsten.infura.io/v3/39180531508b4b659780ef7a36426a86 🖑

wss://ropsten.infura.io/ws/v3/39180531508b4b659780ef7a36426a86 🗐

Figure 11-1. *Infura project keys*

Use this endpoint as a parameter for the Web3 object constructor.
In the Program.cs file, get the balance from Web3 using your wallet's
public address as a parameter. Write the code to output the balance in
wei and then convert the wei balance to ether. Finally, write the code
to output the balance in ether. Now, change your main method to call
GetAccountBalance().

```
using System;
using System.Threading.Tasks;
using Nethereum.Web3;

namespace NethereumSample
{
    class Program
    {
        static void Main(string[] args)
        {
            GetAccountBalance().Wait();
            Console.ReadLine();
        }
```

```
    static async Task GetAccountBalance()
    {
        var web3 = new Web3("https://ropsten.infura.io/
                v3/39180531508b4b659780ef7a36426a86");
        var balance = await web3.Eth.GetBalance.SendRequest
                Async("0x03d1b3162DBFaB4A175038eAa4EA
                4b39423d5A6F");
        Console.WriteLine($"Balance in Wei: {balance.Value}");

        var etherAmount = Web3.Convert.FromWei(balance.Value);
        Console.WriteLine($"Balance in Ether: {etherAmount}");
    }
  }
}
```

Getting the Balance

Build the project. This command builds a project and all of its dependencies:

```
$ dotnet build
```

Run the project. This command runs the source code without any explicit compile or launch commands:

```
$ dotnet run
```

Check the terminal output and make sure that you get the result shown in Figure 11-2.

Figure 11-2. *VS code balances in wei and ether*

Summary

In this chapter, you learned how to create a console project that gets a wallet balance using Nethereum.

CHAPTER 12

Conclusion

During the course of this book I presented the most common use cases for the blockchain today in a simple manner. The idea was to keep it simple and get straight to the point. All the examples provided in this book were created to make you advance quickly down the learning path. As a developer, I know that the best way to learn is by coding, so I wanted to share that way of learning with you.

Learning how to be a blockchain developer is challenging. This is an area that is constantly changing, and staying up-to-date as a professional will take you many hours and a lot of effort. Don't let it be overwhelming for you. We all start from scratch and learn new skills with baby steps. I hope this book gave you the knowledge you need to get started.

With this knowledge, you can now create your own cryptocurrency or create your own NFT and put it up for sale on OpenSea, or better yet, you can host your first site on IPFS with a custom domain in ENS. You can also query off-chain data using Chainlink oracles or use Filecoin to preserve data in a distributed fashion. The possibilities are endless.

Remember, the blockchain is gaining traction, and it's no longer limited to Bitcoin and Ethereum. In the future, we will see lots of projects growing and others losing space. But never forget that technology exists to solve real problems. To apply what you learned in this book, think first about what problems you are trying to solve and whether they are best solved with off-chain solutions. At the end of the day, the blockchain will help you solve problems related to trust. Is a centralized data source trustworthy? Is a centralized application trustworthy? If not, go with the blockchain.

© Davi Pedro Bauer 2022

D. P. Bauer, *Getting Started with Ethereum*, https://doi.org/10.1007/978-1-4842-8045-4_12

I hope you enjoyed reading this book; last but not least, never stop learning. I hope to see you soon as a blockchain developer.

Here are some references for further reading:

- OpenSea[1]

- OpenSea Testnets[2]

- Rinkeby Authenticated Faucet[3] (social validation)

- Rinkeby Ether Faucet[4] (no social validation)

- Matic Faucet[5]

- Polygon Faucet[6]

- IPFS documentation[7]

- Filecoin documentation[8]

- Filecoin Lotus[9]

- Truffle, Filecoin[10]

- Ethereum Name Service[11]

- Chainlink documentation[12]

- Nethereum documentation[13]

---

[1] https://opensea.io

[2] https://testnets.opensea.io

[3] https://faucet.rinkeby.io

[4] http://rinkeby-faucet.com

[5] https://faucet.matic.network

[6] https://matic.supply

[7] https://docs.ipfs.io

[8] https://docs.filecoin.io

[9] https://docs.filecoin.io/get-started/lotus/

[10] https://www.trufflesuite.com/docs/filecoin/truffle/quickstart

[11] https://ens.domains/

[12] https://docs.chain.link

[13] http://docs.nethereum.com/en/latest/

Index

A, B

Blockchain Developer Kit, 3, 4, 126

C

Chainlink Oracles
    contracts package, 108
    decentralized network, 107
    deployment, 116
    Infura project, 112, 113
    migration file, 111, 112
    network configuration, 114
    price feeds, 110
    price information, 117
    private key, 115, 116
    project creation, 108
    seed phrase, 116
    sign transactions, 113, 114
    smart contract, 108, 116
    solidity compiler, 115
    VS Code contracts folder, 109

D

Docker's techniques, 3

E

Ethereum Name Service (ENS), 103
    crypto/tokens/NFT, 103
    domain registration page, 105
    domains page, 104
    registration page, 104
    resolution name, 106
Ethereum Virtual Machine (EVM)
    Blockchain Developer Kit, 3, 4
    description, 1
    Docker, 2
    Ganache, 6, 7
    gas, 2
    MetaMask, 7–11
    Truffle, 4–6
    Visual Studio Code, 2

F

Faucets
    description, 75
    ether testing, 77, 78
    Polygon, 80, 81
    rETH, 76, 77
    TestToken/MATIC-ETH, 78, 79

Printed in the United States
by Baker & Taylor Publisher Services

Printed in the United States
by Baker & Taylor Publisher Services